NMu/ff

Adobe Edge Animate

Using Web Standards to Create Interactive Websites

Please return / renew by date shown.
You can renew at: **norlink.norfolk.gov.uk**
or by telephone: **0344 800 8006**
Please have your library card & PIN ready.

NORFOLK LIBRARY
AND INFORMATION SERVICE
NORFOLK

D1382274

Simon Widjaja

Adobe Edge Animate

**Using Web Standards to Create
Interactive Websites**

Translation by Susan Spies

Simon Widjaja (http://simonwidjaja.com)
Publisher: Gerhard Rossbach
Project Editor and Copyeditor: Maggie Yates
Proofreader: Carey Hobart
Translation: Susan Spies
Layout: Jan Martí, Command Z
Cover Design: Helmut Kraus (www.exclam.de)
Printer: Friesens
Printed in Canada

ISBN 978-1-937538-25-5

1st Edition 2014
© 2014 by Simon Widjaja

Rocky Nook Inc.
802 East Cota St., 3rd Floor
Santa Barbara, CA 93103
www.rockynook.com

Copyright © 2014 by dpunkt.verlag GmbH, Heidelberg, Germany.
Title of the German original: Lebendige Webseiten mit Adobe Edge Animate
ISBN: 978-3-86490-025-9
Translation Copyright © 2013 by Rocky Nook. All rights reserved.

Library of Congress Cataloging-in-Publication Data

Widjaja, Simon.
  Adobe Edge animate : using Web standards to create interactive websites / by Simon Widjaja.
     pages cm
  ISBN 978-1-937538-25-5 (paperback : alkaline paper)
  1. Adobe Edge animate (Computer file) 2. Computer animation. 3. Web sites--Design. 4. Interactive multimedia.
  I. Title.
  TR897.72.A34W53 2013
  006.6'96--dc23
                        2013028536

Distributed by O'Reilly Media
1005 Gravenstein Highway North
Sebastopol, CA 95472

All rights reserved. No part of the material protected by this copyright notice may be reproduced or utilized in any form, electronic or mechanical, including photocopying, recording, or by any information storage and retrieval system, without written permission of the publisher.

Many of the designations in this book used by manufacturers and sellers to distinguish their products are claimed as trademarks of their respective companies. Where those designations appear in this book, and Rocky Nook was aware of a trademark claim, the designations have been printed in caps or initial caps. All product names and services identified throughout this book are used in editorial fashion only and for the benefit of such companies with no intention of infringement of the trademark. They are not intended to convey endorsement or other affiliation with this book.

While reasonable care has been exercised in the preparation of this book, the publisher and author(s) assume no responsibility for errors or omissions, or for damages resulting from the use of the information contained herein or from the use of the discs or programs that may accompany it.

This book is printed on acid-free paper.

Foreword

"Yet another banner design tool?" That was the initial reaction of many web designers when Adobe introduced its new animation tool in August 2011. The first public preview was like a blast from the past, going back to the web animation classic, Flash 4. But the development pace of what Adobe produced was (and continues to be) impressive. The program's real potential became clear in Previews 3 and 4 with the introduction of symbols and interactive features. Not only does Edge Animate produce fully standard-compliant code, the output is also based on the popular JavaScript library, jQuery, which opens the door to extensibility. The general knowledge base for web animation and current jQuery plug-ins can easily be used with Edge Animate so that designers or coders only need to use the core functions of Edge Animate, plus certain workarounds, to create compatiblity under new web standards. With this approach in mind, I have plunged into many experiments, tunneled down into Edge Animate, and created extensions with many libraries and frameworks that I will share in this book.

Cologne, spring 2013
Simon Widjaja

Contents

1

Introduction

1 Introduction

✎ **Adobe Says Thanks**
Adobe would like to thank the community for providing important feedback. Adobe has made the first version of Edge Animate free of charge. License fees will be charged starting with the second version.

✎ **A Note From the Publisher**
This book was originally published in German. Because some of the screenshots were made using German programs, certain images may still contain some German language. However, anything that is pertinent to explaining the information being presented has been translated into English.

Static websites and boring screens full of text have been obsolete for some time now. Clients now expect their websites to have an attractive interface packed with impressive effects, including simple transitions and complex animations. Thanks to Adobe Flash technology, this past decade, web designers were able to pull out all the stops in the field of web animation design. With the introduction of new features, such as the canvas element or CSS3 transitions, HTML5 and CSS3 now offer easy ways to create interactive animations. While the creative coding community is already diligently experimenting with animation libraries and frameworks and producing impressive results, visual-based web designers and animators are still in the starting blocks for lack of professional tools. Creative giant Adobe wants to change this with the new tool, Edge Animate, which exclusively outputs code based on open web standards, for interactive animations. As is the usual practice for Adobe, the creative community was involved in the development process from a very early point. This enabled Adobe to make sure that Edge Animate was tailored to the needs of its target user group as much as possible. Such involvement also gave users the chance to integrate the tool in their work at an early stage and notify Adobe about bugs or feature requests. It was a complete win-win situation, thanks to Adobe's conscious efforts to establish a very agile development strategy. In seven public previews, Adobe gave users an in-depth look at the application. While the first previews were limited to simple animations, the final version allowed for complex and nested animations using symbols, numerous interactivity features and even the integration of web fonts. The time has come to take a closer look at this promising authoring tool.

1.1 What This Book Is About

Edge Animate is a multimedia authoring tool based on open web standards. These are now very common and no longer restricted solely to the browser. Compositions created with Edge Animate can be used in browser applications and apps on mobile devices, but also in digital publications created with Adobe Digital Publishing Suite or Apple iBooks Author. To help you with designing and creating animations in Edge Animate, and to show you solutions that go beyond the application's standard functions, the chapters of the book are organized as follows:

▸ **Chapter 1: Introduction** • You will receive the basic information on the current status quo in web standards that applies to understanding Edge Animate and its usage.

▸ **Chapter 2: Getting to know the authoring tool** • This chapter will take you on a tour of the Edge Animate interface and its many functions. This section will also discuss the program's various user groups and areas of use.

▸ **Chapter 3: Design** • Here you will explore the functions for creating graphic elements within Edge Animate, learn how to use various assets (images and fonts) and create more complex layouts.

▸ **Chapter 4: Animation** • This section will introduce you to the Timeline and the Pin, and teach you how to animate your compositions using keyframes.

▸ **Chapter 5: Interaction** • In this chapter, you will get to know the Edge Animate API and learn how to implement various actions.

▸ **Chapter 6: Publication** • This chapter deals with the various publishing options available to you in Edge Animate and explains the necessary preparations (e.g., Preloader) for publishing your composition on the web or within a digital publication. You will also learn how your creative work can be integrated into a content management system.

▸ **Chapter 7: Advanced tips** • Once you have learned the core functions of Edge Animate, this chapter will send you off with a range of extensions you will need to make your projects perform well on the web.

> ✎ **Digital Publishing Suite**
> DPS is an InDesign-based application for creating digital publications for tablets such as the iPad. The program also uses HTML5 to create articles, which opens the door for creating compositions in Edge Animate.
>
> ✎ **iBooks Author**
> Apple created iBooks Author as a competitor to Adobe DPS. The program lets you create publications for the iBookstore.

1.2   Moving Target: Open Web Standards

HTML5 is one of the many buzzwords currently dominating the web coding and design community. But HTML5 actually means more than just the next generation of open markup language. HTML5 often refers to the entire set of open web standards such as HTML, CSS and JavaScript, which can be deceptive. Although the trio is already being called the web standard, the latest versions of all three technologies have not yet been adopted as a standard. For example, HTML5 will supposedly only receive recommendation status from the W3C (World Wide Web Consortium) in 2014. Even though these are still works in progress, most of the new features are already supported in modern browsers like Firefox, Chrome, Safari or Internet Explorer 9/10. This information is important in order to understand why Edge Animate does not entirely support certain functions. Audio playback is a very good example. While HTML5 can play sound files, the difference in results across browsers is still so major that a simple sound integration is not possible without extra steps. Before offering an incomplete solution, Adobe has intentionally avoided this function for the time being. We can definitely expect to see support for sound integration once the browser problems become less of an issue. However, until that happens, you can use other libraries, such as SoundJS or Edge Commons, to implement the missing functions on your own.

✎ **HTML5: Current Version**
The current version of HTML5 specifications can be found on the official website of the W3C: http://www.w3.org/standards/about.html

1.3   Web Animations: Status Quo

Some of the newly introduced functions in HTML5 and CSS3 offer many new possibilities in web animation, compared to previous versions. With the above-mentioned canvas tag and the CSS rules, many effects can be created for transitions and animations that were previously only possible in extra plug-ins like the Flash Player. Meanwhile, there are many graphics and animation libraries in JavaScript extensions available to the creative coder:

▸ CreateJS (http://createjs.com)
▸ raphaelJS (http://raphaeljs.com)
▸ GSAP JS (http://www.greensock.com/gsap-js)

These libraries all have one thing in common: they take a code-driven approach, thus requiring extensive knowledge of JavaScript programming. In comparison, Edge Animate belongs to a new generation and follows a purely visual approach. Using familiar WYSIWYG (What You See Is What You Get) technology, complex animation choreography can be immediately created without constantly thinking it through in code. More tools in this genre are:

▸ Hype (http://tumult.com/hype)
▸ Sencha Animator (http://www.sencha.com/products/animator)

2

Authoring Tool

2 Authoring Tool Adobe Edge Animate

Now that you have a taste for the advantages of open web standards in the field of web animations, this chapter will give you a closer look at the authoring tool, Adobe Edge Animate, and explain how you can use the program in your regular creative workflow. Only those who truly master the tools of the trade can optimize workflows, work in interdisciplinary teams and deliver results when faced with unusual demands. On the following pages, not only will we cover the installation of the software step by step, we will also look at Edge Animate from the perspective of different types of user groups. With the software's many potential applications in mind, you will learn about the different panels and how to control animation and scripting functions. I will also go over pertinent background information on Edge Animate Runtime that you will need to unleash your creativity.

2.1   User Groups

Unlike other media, such as radio, TV, or print, the web (particularly interactive animations and user interfaces) has one very distinctive feature—it combines a variety of disciplines. Online productions are a cross between visual design and technology-driven programming, in which factors such as usability and user experience play a very central role. The environment around Adobe is a melting pot of creative developers. For nearly a decade, the Adobe Flash ecosystem was the first point of contact for web designers who wanted to create more than just lifeless websites cluttered with monotonous text. Anyone who wanted to produce stunning, interactive websites had a hard time without the Flash plug-in solution. For a long time, the Flash scene was a pivotal point for creative programmers who constantly tried to define the limits of what was possible. The open web standards for HTML5, CSS3 and JavaScript have caught up and their higher availability and compatibility make them a better alternative to the Flash Platform for many scenarios. Edge Animate is one of the flagships of the new Adobe web platform, and the focus was on its relevant user groups, which can roughly be defined as follows:

2.1.1   (Web) Motion Designers, Interface/Interaction Designers, Web Designers, Former Flash Designers

Types of projects: Animated films, online presentations, microsites with static content and banners

Additional tools: Adobe Creative Suite including Photoshop, Illustrator and Fireworks

There is no doubt that this is the main user group. It includes designers and animators with some scripting capabilities. This group is familiar with Timeline-based programs such as Flash Professional, After Effects, Premiere, Final Cut, Motion, or Cinema 4D. In this field, animations are often stand-alone components and seldom entail connections to external systems such as Content Management Systems (CMS). Visual design and storytelling are the clear priorities.

2.1.2   Graphic/Print Designers Who Want to Expand Their Web Design Services

Types of projects: Banners, simple online presentations and microsites with static content

Additional tools: Adobe Creative Suite including Photoshop, Illustrator and Fireworks

Edge Animate is ideal for web novices because it is primarily a graphical interface for the animation of assets (images, graphics, text, etc.) and only requires the use of a few simple steps to create interactivity. Anyone comfortable with editing digital images and who has a knack for typography and layouts will be creating strong web content in no time with Edge Animate.

2.1.3   E-Publication Producers

Types of projects: All types of e-publications (e-magazines, portfolios, etc.)

Additional tools: Adobe Digital Publishing Suite and Adobe Creative Suite, especially InDesign

In addition to e-books, e-magazines and portfolios—digital formats based on traditional print media—are becoming very important. Animations, interactivity, and multimedia content also play a central role here, making Edge Animate the perfect tool. The Adobe Digital Publishing Suite (DPS) offers several extensions for the classic page layout program InDesign, thus facilitating the integration of content based on open standards. It comes as no surprise that Edge Animate offers various export options for this scenario. In addition to the Digital Publishing Suite, Edge Animate also supports Apple's iBook format.

2.1.4   Web Designers and Developers

Types of projects: Templates for content management systems, complicated user interfaces that are built out in a second stage through programming

Additional tools: JavaScript libraries, frameworks, various APIs and possibly other code editors / IDEs

This user group approaches web animation from a more technical perspective and sets aside Edge Animate only when the animation reaches a certain degree of complexity. For example, simple movements and transition animations are usually manually coded, such as with jQuery, which hardly makes sense for large animation sequences. These can be created in Edge Animate compositions with templates, which the designer or developer then codes to create a specific function. Components such as jQuery UI can be added and different programming interfaces (APIs), such as the Facebook API, can be docked to the composition.

What all user groups share is the output media of websites, mobile apps, and television. Since most web workers have many talents and the line between design and development is often blurred in many areas, there is some overlap between the different user groups.

2.2 Applications and Workflows

Like the user groups, there is just as much variety in the scenarios in which Edge Animate is used. The following examples will give you a rough idea of what is possible with Edge Animate.

2.2.1 Edge Animate Banners

The most rudimentary products are banners. Banners are used to draw attention to promotions or products, which is often accomplished with simple animations. (Unfortunately, they are often an annoyance to web surfers.) While GIF animations have long been obsolete due to their poor quality, large file size, and lack of interactivity, in recent years banners were often created as Flash movies. However, because these do not run in every system and can easily be circumvented with ad-blocking software, Edge Animate will likely play a big role in future banner production. Due to their short shelf life and rudimentary qualities, Edge Animate banners are modest compositions with little to no interaction.

2.2.2 Edge Animate for Storytelling

Edge Animate is perfect for telling stories that are viewable on almost all platforms and devices. Although the first version of Edge Animate is missing a few important features, such as path animations, it can create extensive animation sequences in a simple manner, suitable for applications such as eLearning, games, and product presentations.

Figure 2.1
Edge Animate is the perfect tool for storytelling

2.2.3   Edge Animate on Mobile Devices

Since Edge Animate's final output is based exclusively on open standards, which can be displayed on all smartphones and tablets, you will have no problem publishing your productions on mobile devices. Of course, you must account for the more limited features of the device. Especially regarding user interaction, it is important to watch all the bells and whistles, such as multi-touch gestures, and make adjustments to the composition when necessary to create a positive user experience.

Figure 2.2
Edge Animate animations can be played on almost all modern smartphones and tablets

2.2.4   Edge Animate and DPS

When creating compositions specifically for use on tablets, the Digital Publishing Suite for InDesign is an exciting option. The program lets you create visually rich and interactive e-magazines as if you were working in InDesign. Edge Animate offers special export features for use in the DPS-environment so that your compositions can be seamlessly imported into InDesign.

2.2.5   Embedding Edge Animate in Other Pages or CMS

Of course, you do not always have to create the entire website in Edge Animate. You can also use the program for individual elements such as a slide show, an animated header, or even just a more complex menu. Because Edge Animate only exports code based on open standards, you can easily integrate an Edge Animate composition into other pages or a CMS (content management system).

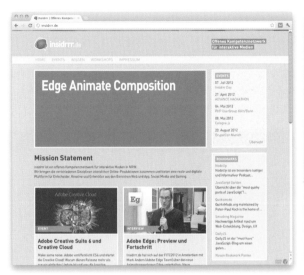

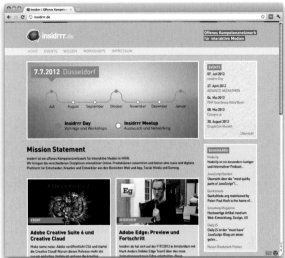

Figure 2.3
Edge Animate compositions can be integrated into any HTML document. Here is an animation within a block of the Drupal content management system.

2.3   Download and Installation

You can download the current version of Edge Animate as part of the 30-day free trial of Adobe Creative Cloud at http://creative.adobe.com

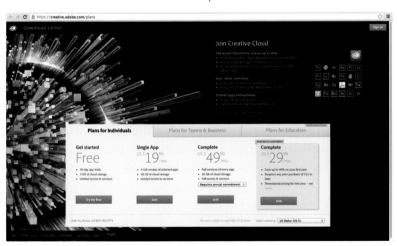

After registration, you can download and install both Edge Animate and Edge Code for free. The second release of Edge Animate will likely be offered as an individual software program for purchase, and as part of the Creative Cloud.

2.4 User Interface

Edge Animate is a visual authoring tool that greatly simplifies the creative work-flow through a context-sensitive user interface. In classical WYSIWYG fashion, the user immediately sees the results and can navigate to all corresponding settings for a selected object. A two-monitor system can be an advantage depending on the display size, number of layers, and the complexity of the animations.

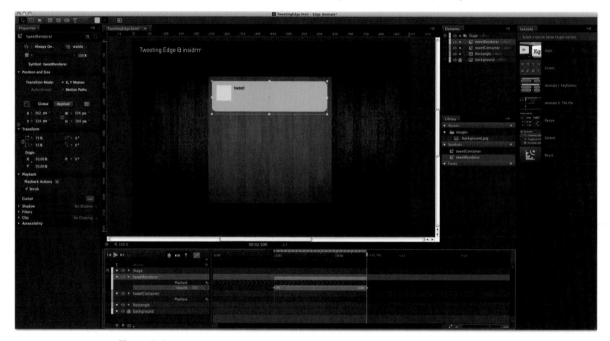

Figure 2.4

The Edge Animate interface offers quick access to all relevant functions through its many panels

The program interface is similar to other animation tools, such as Adobe Flash Professional or the classic Adobe After Effects motion graphic software. However, Adobe Edge is considerably closer to Flash Professional in terms of the scope of functions (interactivity) and output medium (web). Anyone familiar with the Flash authoring tool will be a quick study with Edge Animate.

Figure 2.5
Adobe Flash Professional (left) and
After Effects (right)

Before we start with a first small animation, let's take a closer look at the individual panels of the user interface.

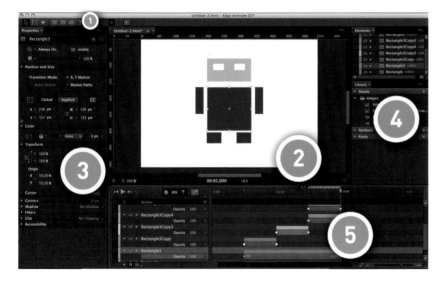

Figure 2.6
The user interface of Edge Animate
with its panels, the Stage, and Timeline

1. Tools panel
2. Stage
3. Property panel
4. Elements and Library
5. Timeline with keyframes

2.4.1 Getting Started Panel

After you open Edge Animate, you are offered several start options. On the left side you can open an existing Edge Animate project, create an empty project, or reopen a recent file. The right side offers information and links to resources as well as a number of in-app sample projects that are the perfect introduction for Edge Animate newcomers. The lesson contents are presented with text and images in a separate panel within Edge Animate so that you can immediately apply what you are learning right in the UI. You have the option to go through all points one by one or skip ahead to the lesson's output and explore it on your own.

Figure 2.7

The lessons are straightforward sample compositions that use text and images to explain the basics step by step in a separate panel

2.4.2 Tools Panel

The main Tools panel in the first version of Edge Animate is still quite modest. This is because most animation elements are placed on the Stage through the Import dialog or by a direct drag-and-drop. Edge Animate currently offers very limited features for creating new shapes.

The first group controls how the mouse selects and modifies elements. The first icon, the Selection Tool, is used to select elements. In normal selection mode, you can resize elements by single-clicking and dragging the corner control points without distorting the proportions of any existing sub-elements. If the second icon on the Tools panel is activated, you are in transform mode. In this mode, the element, including whatever it contains (text, etc.), is changed (rotated, scaled, skewed) when its corner control points are moved. The third icon activates the clipping mode, used to clip or mask graphic elements. If only part of a graphic element should be visible, it can be selected by clipping it. In this process, the visible section can be changed via the control point, or the image content within this section can be moved around to any position.

The next four icons are used to create simple basic shapes, basically DIV containers (HTML) with various visual attributes and text containers. The three options for DIV containers are identical except for the corner radius. The corner radius can be adjusted at a later time by entering a value in the corresponding property field or by selecting the Transform Tool to adjust using the control points.

The three remaining buttons are used for filling in and outlining shapes with standard colors. The Layout defaults settings, which are automatically applied to all new elements, can be modified at a later point.

Figure 2.8
The Layout defaults are used to set default settings for coordinates, sizes, and images

2.4.3   The Stage

The Stage is where all creative work in Edge Animate takes place. Here we see the state of our composition at the current position of the playhead. All elements are accurately displayed, except for the execution of scripts. Moreover, all elements that are on the Stage and not explicitly locked can be selected with the mouse. The Stage is a realistic and reliable representation of your work. It is not a simulation but rather an output from the WebKit rendering engine for the display of HTML and CSS data. This actual representation has the advantage that even custom classes of HTML or CSS can be depicted easily.

 WebKit
WebKit is an open source program (engine) for the display of web content, used by many browsers, including Apple, Safari, Google Chrome, and Android.

2.4.4 Property Panel

The Property panel on the left side lets you change the attributes of the selected element on the Stage. The Property panel is context-sensitive and automatically changes for the selected item. For example, select a text box and the Property panel gives you access to the text formatting properties.

If you have not selected an item on the Stage, the panel displays the properties of the Stage. In this case, the Property panel displays the Stage dimensions and overflow behavior as well as settings for a Down-level Stage, a Poster image for incompatible browsers, and the Preloader. These issues are covered in more detail in the Publishing chapter.

You also have the option to use the curly braces ({}) icon to open a script panel for a specific element in which you can add interactivity. All properties that you set here are represented behind the scenes through corresponding HTML or CSS attributes. Hover your mouse over the property to find out which attributes you are actually changing at the HTML/CSS level. A help text will appear with more information.

Figure 2.9
The involved CSS statements are displayed as a tooltip

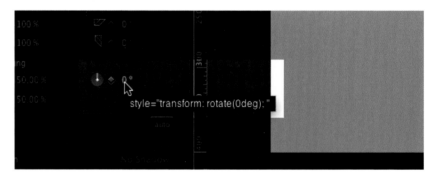

2.4.5 Elements Panel

The Elements panel is a hierarchical view of all existing elements, including the Stage itself. This panel offers you five options. Like in many other Adobe products, such as Photoshop, use the eye icon to make a lane visible and editable and use the dot icon to lock it. These settings only apply to the preview and have no effect on the final result. As a third option, you can change the name of a layer by double-clicking on the name and rearrange the order and nesting of elements by dragging and dropping them in the panel stack. Through the use of nesting, element groups can be created for easier editing without any impact on how the elements will display.

Moreover, you can also directly access the Code panel for the selected element via the curly braces icon to add interactivity. Elements that have already been coded for interactivity are indicated by brighter curly braces, making it easy to see where code has been used.

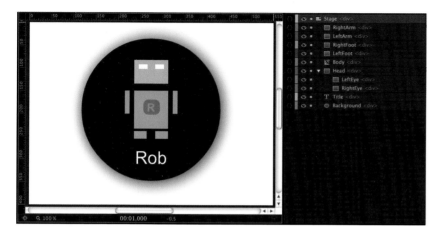

Figure 2.10
The Elements panel shows all elements in the DOM and the associated HTML tag

Because Edge Animate not only exports valid HTML but also works with an HTML document in its development phase, all elements, including basic shapes, graphics, or text, are saved as HTML tags in the DOM (Document Object Model). In other words, the Elements panel is a one-to-one representation of all DOM elements. The icon in front of the element name indicates the type in Edge Animate (shape, image, or text) and the tag after the name indicates the corresponding HTML tag used to represent the element.

2.4.6 Library Panel

The Library panel is located under the Elements panel. This panel groups together all objects that can be referenced. This includes any external images, previously created symbols, and custom fonts. Basic shapes are not included in this list. A symbol is a kind of blueprint or definition for a specific element on the Stage. The actual depicted element on the Stage is called an instance. A symbol definition can have any number of instances on the Stage, whose predefined display can also be entirely changed by overwriting the instance's properties. A symbol definition is also maintained in the Library even if all instances are removed from the Stage. This is because you can trigger an action through code while playing a composition, which automatically creates an instance of a symbol and places it on the Stage.

Symbol definitions can be exported for reuse in other projects. To do this, right-click the symbol in the Library and choose Export. The + icon in the Library panel is used to import symbols into existing compositions.

Figure 2.11

Symbols can also be exported
from the Library for reuse in
other projects

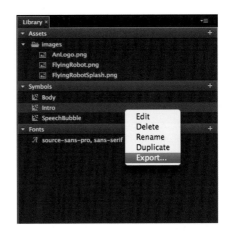

2.4.7   The Timeline

The Timeline is the command central for all animations. The panel gives you a chronological representation of the composition with all set keyframes and animation actions. In the Timeline, the only elements that appear are ones that you either created with Edge Animate or that are already animated, because HTML documents often consist of hundreds of items. Open one such document and you will quickly lose your overview of all the elements involved.

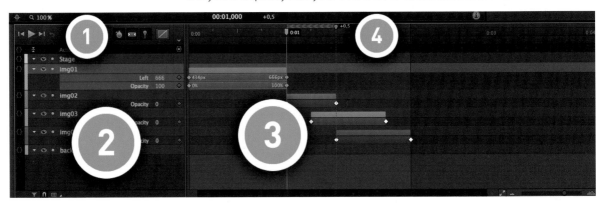

Figure 2.12

The Timeline in Edge Animate
is the command central for all
animations and their keyframes

The Timeline panel is divided into four areas:

1. Controls and options: These controls are for playing the animation, including fast-forwarding and rewinding it. You can also change the behavior of the keyframes. The stopwatch icon activates the Auto-Keyframe Mode, which automatically inserts a keyframe for all changes made to elements on the Stage. The second icon activates the Auto-Transition Mode, which calculates the necessary interpolation between two keyframes, creating the intermediate steps for a smooth transition. Turning that option off creates abrupt changes between keyframes (see section 4.1.1). The pin icon activates the Pin, a second playhead for easy positioning of keyframes for transitions (see section 4.1.1). The grid icon with the diagonal line is used to apply an easing function to a keyframe animation. It opens a dialog box with options and a time/change graph to illustrate the course of the animation.

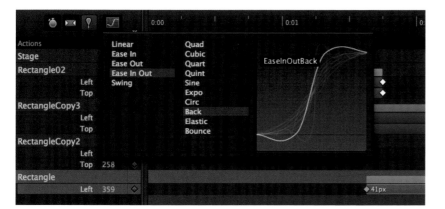

Figure 2.13

Easing functions are non-linear animation sequences that make animations appear more natural, especially when motion is involved

2. Hierarchy of the animated levels: The left section of the Timeline lists the activated levels with their animation actions. Here each property is listed (e.g., opacity, color, width, etc.) on a separate lane. Individual levels can be expanded or collapsed. You can modify keyframes directly from this left section or set new ones. You can also change the values displayed in yellow with the mouse or click the diamond icon to set a new keyframe at the playhead's current position. You can also use the curly braces on the left side to define actions for individual levels. The lower bar of the Timeline contains three other functions for filtering the tracks displayed (filter icon) and controlling snapping on the Timeline (magnet symbol). To facilitate working on the Timeline, you can also display a grid within the Timeline, which is especially useful for fine-tuning keyframes.

3. Keyframes: Here is where the actual choreography takes place. Any element animated over a defined time frame is displayed together with its keyframes as a colored animation track. Clicking one of the tracks displays the starting and ending values so you can view the keyframe's properties. Keyframes can be moved around with the mouse, and animation sequences can be easily transferred to other tracks with copy-and-paste.

Figure 2.14

Animation sequences and keyframes in the Timeline

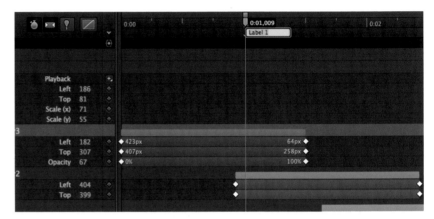

4. Timeline with playhead: The Timeline with playhead is located directly above the keyframes. Use the mouse to move it around and jump within an animation to a certain point. Directly below the Timeline time markers are two other lanes that you might not immediately notice. The upper lane is used for labels. A label is a point on the Timeline that can be jumped to through code. To define such a label, simply move to the desired location and then click on the icon with the down arrow to the left of the lane. A label is solely defined by position and text. For example, the latter can be used in a play statement as follows: `sym.play "Intro")`.

Figure 2.15

Labels and actions enable the creation of nonlinear compositions

Triggers and actions are located in the grey-shaded lane under the labels. This is where you can execute an action; in other words, these are code statements at a specific point on the Timeline. As with elsewhere in Edge Animate, code statements are displayed here in curly braces. Using the diamond-shaped keyframe icons, you can assign this code to a specific point in time. These particular types of actions are called triggers. To create a new trigger, click the down arrow icon to the left of the lane (like in the Label track above) to open the Code panel.

2.4.8   Workspace

Depending on the workflow and monitor resolution, it is sometimes more practical to arrange the panels differently or temporarily close a specific panel. Use the Window menu to reopen a specific panel. If you frequently change your workspace, choose Window > Workspace to save your preferred panel arrangement or restore the default workspace.

2.4.9   Keyboard Shortcuts

Edge Animate also offers many shortcuts that you can adapt to your own preferences by selecting Edit > Keyboard Shortcuts.

Figure 2.16

The standard Adobe dialog box for setting custom shortcuts

2.5   Hello Edge Animate!

Before we wade in too deeply, it is now time to take Edge Animate for a test drive. Since you have probably already installed and opened Edge Animate, let's create a small animation.

1.   First we create a new composition by choosing File > New.
2.   On the Stage, use the Text Tool (T button) to create a simple text field, enter any text, and change the text properties such as font type, size, and text color to whatever you prefer.

📄 **Project**

The files for this example can be downloaded from http://edgebuch. simonwidjaja.com

Project Name: Authoringtool_Hello

3. Now let's have the text fly from left to right on the Stage. To do this, we need the Timeline and the Pin. First, enable the Pin by pressing the P key on the keyboard so that the blue pin appears directly above the playhead in the Timeline. The Pin is an easy way to create simple animations. It is separated from the playhead and can be moved to any point on the Timeline. Let's do that now by pulling the blue pin to the right until we reach one second (00:01). Now we can specify the starting position of the animation by dragging the previously created text off the Stage to the left. Since Auto-Keyframe Mode is enabled by default, the keyframes have already been created, producing an animation. After each animation, disable the Pin by pressing the P key on the keyboard to avoid any quick creation of unintentional animations when you move elements.

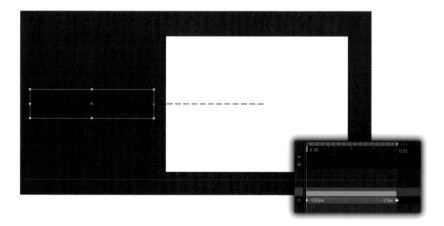

4. Let's apply this process to another text element positioned directly below
    the first text, but have this one float in from the right.

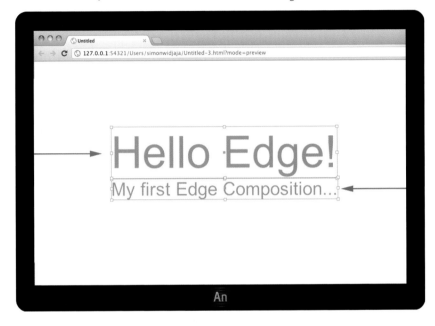

5. Now preview your first animation in the browser with keyboard shortcut
    Cmd/Ctrl + Enter. Violà! You have just created your first animation that you
    can publish on any web server without further editing.

2.6   Edge Animate Runtime Basics

The power of Edge Animate—and also the greatest limitation of the Adobe
Flash Platform—is that it only uses open web standards. The first version of Edge
Animate's software exclusively works with the DOM, in which it places all visual
elements using DIV containers, which are then styled and animated with CSS
and JavaScript.

2.6.1   System Requirements

Because Edge Animate uses HTML5 to create animations, it requires the use
of modern browsers. Projects created in Edge Animate run in Mozilla Firefox,
Google Chrome, Apple Safari and Microsoft Internet Explorer 9+. Internet Explorer 6–8 only offers very limited support of HTML5, so Edge Animate compositions
are only displayed in a minimalist version (see section 6.1.2). Android and iOS
devices use the modern WebKit engine to render HTML content, which can
display Edge Animate content.

2.6.2   HTML & Co.

Given all the hype surrounding HTML5, you would think that Adobe used the HTML5 canvas element in its development of Edge Animate. Surprisingly, this was not the case. First of all, the display of canvas content is still not very good on mobile devices. Moreover, canvas technology is not supported consistently across all browsers. An animation rendered with a canvas element would currently only run on about 67% of all browsers.

🖉 HTML5 Canvas

The canvas element is like a canvas component (bitmap) in HTML that can be drawn using JavaScript.

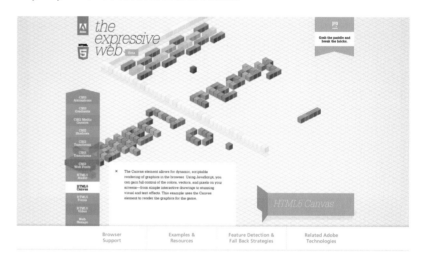

Figure 2.17

The display of content with the HTML5 canvas element is not yet supported due to low browser penetration

The situation is similar to the display of SVG (Scalable Vector Graphics); there is still no consistent market penetration for this type of graphic file. Thus, in the first version of Edge Animate, SVG formats can only be used for the import of static vector graphics. Additional code output with the canvas element or SVG images would be an advantage and is expected to be a part of subsequent versions, as this feature is often requested by the web-design community.

The fact that Edge Animate creates animations in the DOM means that the software does not take full advantage of HTML5. Here the buzzword is being used purely for marketing purposes. Strictly speaking, it is CSS3 and JavaScript that enable you to create lifelike animations with Edge Animate.

Unlike Flash animations, the visual layer of Edge Animate exclusively relies on open web standards so browsers can play animations created in Edge Animate without additional plug-ins. Since Edge Animate output is especially optimized for the WebKit browser engine, you can be sure that your animations will run on mobile devices without any problems. Both iOS (iPhone, iPad and other Apple devices) and Android use WebKit to display web content. Edge Animate especially scores points over Flash in the iOS world following Apple's policy decision to no longer support the playback of Flash content in iOS device browsers.

On one hand, it is good news that content created with Edge Animate no longer requires an additional plug-in. However, there are new hurdles to overcome, and they are anything but minor, given the great variety of available browsers. As long as the browser market does not stabilize and the long-awaited consistency across functions and commands is not achieved, developers and designers will always need to keep a constant eye on the user group and browser differences when using Edge Animate. Edge Animate offers some support through a poster function, including a Down-level Stage so that the animation does not crash the viewer's browser. For non-compatible browsers, at least one static image with the most essential information is displayed.

Since open standards do not allow for any compiling—in other words, no translation into machine code or byte code—all the source code of your user interface and animations (HTML, CSS and JavaScript) are open source and freely viewable to any website visitor. This fact prompts a lot of debate among clients, agencies, and developers. On one hand the open source faction is gaining momentum, but many companies with expensive and elaborate web content want to have more control over their source code. While the Flash compilation process meant that the published SwF file contained unreadable byte code (at least without special additional tools), the world of open standards requires the use of workarounds. Thus, Edge Animate offers a process capable of making all JavaScript code unreadable to the naked eye through a minifying process. The procedure creates the smallest possible file that still contains the original range of functions.

> **✎ Minifying**
> This process is also sometimes referred to obfuscation, since all variable and function names are changed and obscured in the code structure through many transformations. As the name suggests, the minifying process offers yet another advantage: all source code is boiled down to a minimum. This technique replaces meaningful but unnecessarily long code with simple letters, and it removes comments and unnecessary line breaks.

2.6.3 A Solid Foundation: jQuery

The source code generated by Edge Animate is pure JavaScript, and is based on the JavaScript library, jQuery. This fact is not significant for simple animation designers, but the role of jQuery is very important for anyone who wants a look under the hood of Edge Animate to better understand how it functions, and to learn how to enhance it with other components.

jQuery was originally developed to offer uniform access to the visual objects of an HTML document with multi-browser capability. All HTML elements in the browser are stored in the DOM and made available for access, but the syntax for addressing these DOM elements in the various browsers (Internet Explorer, Chrome, Firefox, etc.) is anything but uniform. Without any support, web developers must ensure that their code is correctly implemented for every browser. Thus, jQuery is an abstraction layer that handles this extra and unnecessary work for the web developer. jQuery is the most popular library for handling DOM elements and has earned a strong following among the active web community. The same applies to jQuery's extensions, such as an API for animations and effects, an extensive library of ready-made visual user interface elements (jQuery UI), and even a mobile version, called jQuery Mobile.

Through the use of jQuery, web developers can deploy many additional components and directly apply the available knowledge base within Edge Animate Projects. This makes JavaScript, and especially jQuery, the back door of Edge Animate with which experienced web developers can master challenges that might not be possible with Edge Animate's native tools. Examples include the integration of third-party components, such as calendar forms, playing sound, or linking external content from a CMS.

Since the code created by Edge Animate is exclusively compatible with existing web standards, Edge Animate is not going to reinvent the wheel. Until now, developers needed a lot of heavy coding to create standard-compliant, complex animations, but this workflow will now change dramatically. To that extent, Edge Animate is actually a graphical WYSIWYG interface that significantly simplifies the use of CSS3 properties and jQuery animations.

2.6.4   The Result and Runtime

Since Edge Animate works with HTML and JavaScript documents during the design phase of an animation, it immediately creates the typical file organization for web pages when a new project is created:

Figure 2.18
File organization of an Edge
Animate project

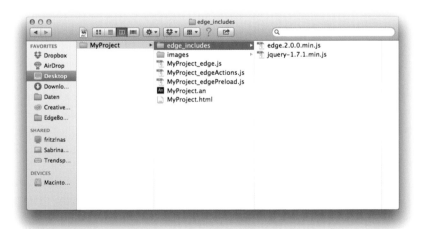

Except for the file with file extension .an, all files are needed for playback of the composition. The file to start the composition is MyProject.html. If you load this file into the browser, the other JavaScript files are loaded as well, and the composition is played back. While the JavaScript files in the first row include the specific project information, the so-called Edge runtime file is contained in the subfolder /edge_includes. This runtime file contains all the code and commands (API) needed to play back the animation. The runtime files are always the same, regardless of the project, and should not be modified in any way. The above-described jQuery is also part of the runtime file, meaning that this file is automatically available in every Edge Animate project.

Theoretically, you can upload the project folder to a web server as is, but this is not recommended since these files are not yet optimized for live use. Rather, Edge Animate offers you various publishing options that optimize the files for different scenarios.

2.6.5   How Code Behaves in Edge Animate

Edge Animate functions in a non-obtrusive manner by accessing and changing existing source code as little as possible. This is a big advantage, and something many web developers greatly appreciate. Many authoring tools with a WYSIWYG interface (such as Adobe Dreamweaver) generate a lot of source code that often does not meet web developer expectations for formatting, scope, and quality, and partially interferes with hand-written code. This is not the case with Edge Animate. All animation information is stored in separate JavaScript files and not mixed in with the rest of the website. For example, if you animate an existing website with Edge Animate, the external animation data is loaded as one JavaScript file into a single block of code. It is loaded into the head section of the HTML document. The syntax is as follows:

```
<!--Adobe Edge Runtime-->
<script type="text/javascript" charset="utf-8"
  src="MyProject_edgePreload.js"></script>
<style>
   .edgeLoad-EDGE-172400391 { visibility:hidden; }
</style>
<!--Adobe Edge Runtime End-->
```

In addition, the existing source code is not modified except for the addition of CSS classes to identify the new elements. This means that after editing in Edge Animate, you can work with the HTML document as usual with any authoring tools.

2.7 Supplementary Tools

Edge Animate is still a very young authoring tool. In the first version, the focus was on the basics of generating compositions and animations, and some of the functionalities were not yet fully developed. For that reason, in some instances it may make sense to use supplementary tools. If you are using the first version, you will probably miss extensive paint tools and a real coding comfort, which can be quite crucial for larger and more ambitious projects. What follows is an overview of the main supplementary programs that can help you in your daily work with Edge Animate.

2.7.1 Design Tools and Image Editing

During both the design phase and post-publishing, only web standards are used to display your compositions. Therefore, you can use any graphic formats common on the Internet. You can also use conventional design tools to visually express your creativity. Edge Animate offers limited tools to create new shapes, so you will probably have to turn to other programs at a very early stage to create JPG, PNG or GIF images, and scalable vector graphics in SVG format. It is important to understand that Edge Animate does not modify the images in an import or export but only links them with CSS statements in the HTML document. This means you should already be thinking about creating graphics that are optimized for display on the Internet. The wrong file format, too large a file size, unnecessary metadata, and poor compression each takes their toll on the final product.

Adobe Photoshop • Adobe Photoshop is indisputably the classic image-editing program. Photoshop is part of the Creative Cloud membership, and provides several export options for the Internet and mobile devices. Photoshop is the right tool whenever you need to create or edit images with a high level of detail, such as photos or structured surfaces with visual effects.

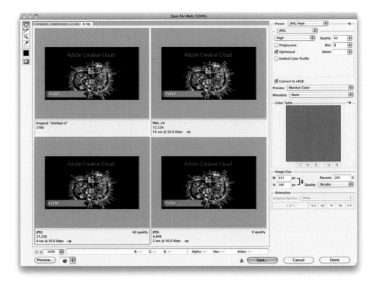

Unfortunately, version 1.5 of Edge Animate does not allow the import of individual layers from a Photoshop PSD file. This would allow you the advantage of creating the static image in Photoshop and saving it as a single file from which Edge Animate could extract whatever elements or levels it needed for the animation. Since this is an obvious benefit, it will certainly be included in future releases. You do not necessarily need to use Photoshop for editing digital images. Any graphic or image-editing program that exports PNG, JPG, or SVG files (such as GIMP) can be used in conjunction with Edge Animate.

Adobe Fireworks · While Photoshop is widely used and offers many ways to export to the web and mobile devices, you don't need to limit your design work to that tool exclusively. Adobe Fireworks, also part of the Creative Cloud, is another tool for creating image data. Unlike Photoshop, the focus in Fireworks is not on the photo-realistic manipulation of images, but rather on the design of user interfaces. Not only does the program offer numerous user functions set up as reusable symbols, but it also provides special features to create application interfaces within the page. For example, you can define different areas within an image and in different states. Even the slicing of compositions into smaller images is much better supported in Fireworks. Another advantage of Fireworks is superior media optimization when exporting image data, yielding better results with smaller file sizes.

✎ Text in Images
If possible, text should be created directly in Edge Animate; this is the only way it is searchable with search engines. If text is part of the image data, it cannot be selected or automatically indexed.

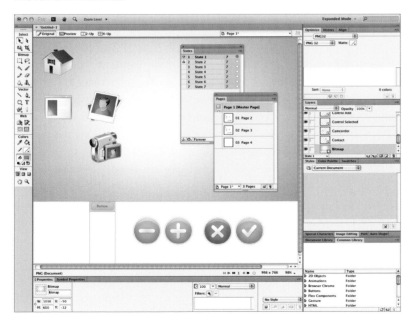

Figure 2.19
Adobe Fireworks has many additional functions for creating web layouts and user interfaces

If you want to use Fireworks in combination with Edge Animate, you should take a look at a Fireworks extension from John Dunning (http://johndunning.com/fireworks/about/EdgeAnimate). This plug-in lets you export your design work from Fireworks into Edge Animate compositions. The extension is still in its beta release, but already performs very well in some application scenarios.

Adobe Illustrator · If you want to create scalable vector graphics, Illustrator is definitely the right choice. This software is also part of the Creative Cloud. It offers a great variety of vector tools and features to create graphics and save them in SVG format. Illustrator has extensive export options, such as naming individual elements within the SVG file, which is ultimately a description file that XML uses to define all graphic elements. Unfortunately, the first version of Edge Animate cannot access the individual elements of an SVG file, meaning that it cannot yet take advantage of this powerful Illustrator feature. This option is also on the wish list for future versions.

2.7.2   Code Editors and IDEs

Since Edge Animate has already been using open web standards in its design phase and saves all project information in JavaScript or HTML files, you do not necessarily have to use Edge Animate's built-in code editor for coding. There are three files that you can edit with a different editor as needed:

▶ PROJECTNAME.html: The main document with basic HTML codes. Here you can add additional JavaScript libraries or CSS style sheets to the header like you can in any other HTML document. You can also easily make changes to the body. For example, it may be necessary to modify the body tag with CSS so that your Edge Animate project is centered on the web page.
▶ PROJECTNAME_edgeActions.js: All actions from your project are saved in this JavaScript file. If you are doing heavy coding and want the convenience of an advanced development environment for extensive JavaScript coding (code completion, snippets, debugging, etc.), use this file as a starting point and edit with any JavaScript editor. In an anonymous function, all actions are defined with the following syntax:

```
Symbol.bindElementAction(compId, symbolName,
    "${_MySymbol}", "click", function(sym, e){
        // Insert code for mouseclick here
});
//Edge binding end
```

▸ PROJECTNAME_edge.js: This file is a little more advanced because it manages the entire structure of the composition, meaning all basic shapes and symbols, as well as external images and fonts. JavaScript is also used here to describe the composition. Elements such as generic objects and arrays are nested in the variable symbols to describe the structure of the symbols and their Timelines. You can ignore this file in your normal workflow since Edge Animate gives you a perfect user interface for creating this file organization. However, editing this file may be useful for creating template projects or similar tasks. You should be very careful if you change something, because you run the risk that the project will no longer open in Edge Animate.

When these files are modified outside of Edge Animate, Edge Animate notifies you of these changes when you come back to the program. You then have the option to accept these changes or discard them. In this way, you can easily use a PingPong workflow to switch back and forth between tools.

Edge Code or Brackets • Brackets is Adobe's streamlined code editor—web-standard compliant and open source. The project is still in its infancy, but already offers enormous potential, partly because the entire editor has been developed with web standards. This means that anyone who knows HTML, CSS, and JavaScript can build with this editor. "Edge Code" is the name of the new editor in Adobe's Edge Tools & Services. This is the basic version of Brackets; it includes various extensions and is available from Adobe as a web design program. For more information on using Edge Code or Brackets, see chapter 5.

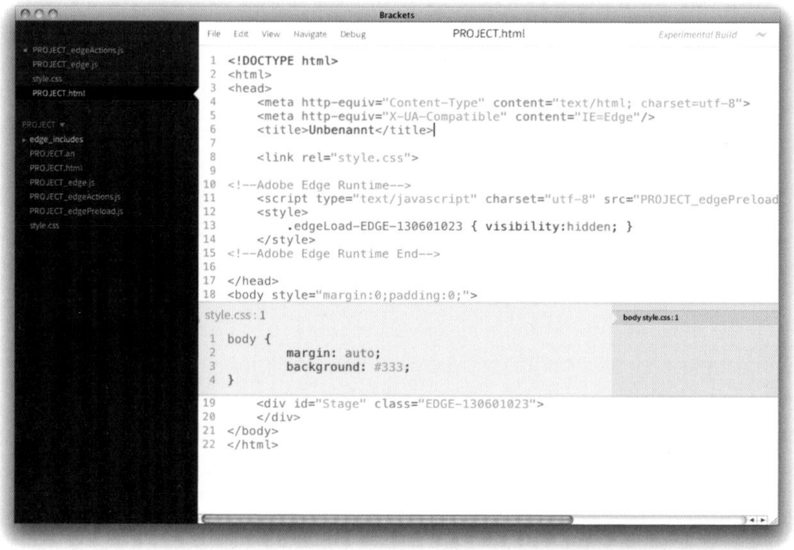

Figure 2.20

Brackets is an editor that
holds great promise—it is
open source and exclusively
built on standards

Figure 2.20
Brackets is an editor that holds great promise—it is open source and exclusively built on standards

Adobe Dreamweaver • In addition to the Flash platform, Adobe has a long tradition in HTML through its powerful development environment for HTML-based websites and web applications as part of the Creative Suite. Adobe Dreamweaver not only offers a variety of tools for programming and a very sophisticated WYSIWYG Design view, but also many extra features like a built-in FTP manager or the PhoneGap Build for creating and publishing hybrid applications.

There still isn't any enhanced support for Edge Animate compositions, but Dreamweaver can be a very useful supplement for code-heavy projects.

JetBrains PhpStorm/WebStorm • If Brackets or Dreamweaver is not enough for you, definitely take a look at PhpStorm or WebStorm. Real code fanatics will get their fill with these. Both Storms are nearly unbeatable for their coding assistance, refactoring, debugging capabilities, and GIT/SVN integration. These are programs for anyone wanting to develop everything from simple actions to complex prototypes, class constructions with complex logic, and even the PHP backend needed for Edge Animate compositions.

3 Creation

3   Creation

On the stage of a theatrical production as well as in real life, the actors play a crucial role and contribute significantly to the success or failure of a choreographed performance. An animation or motion design is no different. The overall impression of an animation largely depends on the quality and expressiveness of the individual visual elements. Pixelated graphics and inconsistent color compositions can disappoint the viewer, even in the most elaborate animations and effects. Before we turn to actual animation and interaction, we will first focus on the topic of designing an animation. In the following pages, you will learn what types of elements are used in Edge Animate and how to set them. When creating a new Edge Animate project, you must choose from two different starting points. You can choose to start from scratch with a blank document and then create elements using the paint tools, or you can import external graphics and images. In the design phase, Edge Animate writes code as HTML, CSS, and JavaScript in the relevant files, so you can also start with an existing HTML document. Edge Animate uses WebKit to render the Stage and all its visual elements, ensuring an accurate depiction of all elements.

Let us have a closer look at the two different starting methods before we zoom in on the Property panel for modifying various object properties.

3.1   Starting From Scratch (Blank Document)

In most cases, you will be starting with a blank document to fill in an entire web page or a portion of an existing website with animations. In both cases, the composition size is usually clear from the get-go. If you want to start with an empty Stage, select Create New on the Getting Started panel.

Once the empty Stage appears, set the width and height of the composition in the Property panel to the left. If you are creating a composition with a flexible layout; in other words, no fixed width and/or height for the Stage, section 3.9 explains the options Edge Animate currently offers for responsive design. Besides the size of the Stage, you can also change the background color, the overflow behavior (see section 3.4.4) and set the option for automatic playback. The composition ID is not an issue at this point, and only becomes relevant when you want to place several Edge Animate compositions in the same website. Moreover, the Down-level Stage, Poster and Preloader fields only become important when publishing the final composition. You will learn about these in chapter 6.

Figure 3.1

You have now created a general structure for the composition. It is recommended that you save projects often to avoid any loss of data.

Now you can start with actual design. The Edge Animate shape tools let you create basic shapes. The application offers three container shapes (DIV container), all of which are simple rectangles. Only the settings for corner rounding vary among the three shape-creating tools, ranging from rectangles with right-angle corners to circles. The default settings for rounded corners can, of course, be edited at a later point and modified individually or all at once. In addition, the application provides a Text tool to create multiple-line text blocks and other text elements. Unfortunately, free-form paths or even three-dimensional elements cannot be created at this time.

Figure 3.2
The drawing and text tools in Edge
Animate are still quite rudimentary

Of course, in addition to the basic shapes, you can also import standard graphics file formats. Since Edge Animate exclusively relies on open web standards, only formats viewable in HTML can be imported. For pixel-based images, you can import JPG, PNG and GIF formats. If you want to use scalable, resource-saving vector graphics, you can also use SVG graphics. External custom fonts can also be added in Edge Animate. You will learn more about this in section 3.8.

Figure 3.3
In addition to common image formats,
vector graphics and fonts can also be
embedded

These image formats can be imported into the Edge Animate Library through the File > Import dialog or dragged directly onto the Stage from the computer's file system.

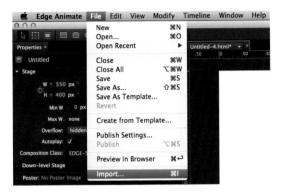

3.2 Elements and the Library

As we mentioned, Edge Animate uses HTML to display content. This means that an HTML tag is created in the background for every item placed on the Stage. The various HTML tags can be nested in any order to form groups, which ultimately creates a DOM or a hierarchical tree structure. This DOM tree is displayed in the Elements panel. Here, all the elements that are actually on the Stage are listed. In contrast, the Library lists all external assets, regardless of whether or not they have already been placed on the Stage. Objects not yet positioned on the Stage are not loaded into the browser when the animation is played since they are not used in the DOM. Symbols are an exception and are loaded in any case, even if they have not been used within the project. This is because symbols may be placed dynamically at runtime via script actions on the Stage.

Figure 3.4

Overview of all the elements/layers and the Library with all available assets

The order of the elements effects how they are displayed in the DOM tree. Elements lower down are behind the elements higher up along the z-axis. Of course, you can also change the order of elements at any time. You can bring an object to the front or send it to the back by right-clicking on an element or element group and selecting Arrange from the context menu. The DOM tree is rearranged to reflect the order you choose. You can also rearrange individual elements by dragging them up and down the DOM tree.

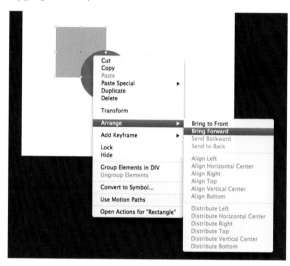

Figure 3.5
Choose Arrange from the context menu to rearrange overlapping elements

The tag next to the element name (e.g. `<div>`) shows which specific tag is used to display that element in the DOM. Usually this information is not necessarily important. However, in some scenarios, such as for SEO, the tag can play an important role. For example, you can choose from the following tags for text elements in the Property panel:

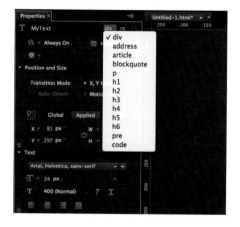

Figure 3.6
You can select the HTML tag for text elements

For images, you can choose either the default DIV or the IMG tag. There are no other alternatives available for shapes and symbols.

3.3 Starting With an HTML Document

You do not necessarily have to start an Edge Animate project with a blank page. Since Edge Animate already uses HTML and JavaScript during the creation of projects, and the Stage uses WebKit to display this data, you can open virtually any HTML document in Edge Animate and then animate it. The only restriction is that it must be a static HTML document; in other words, content not generated by JavaScript or server-side operations, such as PHP. Thus, a web page can be created in Dreamweaver or any other WYSIWYG or code editor. Then the individual elements, such as the header of the website, can be animated in Edge Animate. Here, the original HTML code is basically not modified, which is very important for subsequent editing. The following example demonstrates this approach and clarifies the modifications made by Edge Animate.

As an example, we will use an HTML page with a rather manageable structure. That way we can let a simple header graphic drop in from above and we can show or hide individual elements by changing the opacity. The following screenshot shows the HTML document with the animation being created:

Project

The files for this example can be downloaded from http://edgebuch. simonwidjaja.com
Project Name:
Creation_Startingpoint_HTML

Figure 3.7
Use any HTML document as a starting point

The underlying source code of the HTML document is as follows (slightly shortened for better readability):

```
<!DOCTYPE ...>
 ...
<body>
<div id="content">
    <div id="header">
    <img src="images/logo.png" width="190" height="51" />
    </div>
    <div id="animation">
        <img src="images/animation_title.png" />
    </div>
    <article>
      <div class="article-image">
        <img src="images/insidrrr_blog_creativecloud.jpg"
            width="332" height="180" />
    </div>
    <div class="article-title">
        Adobe Creative Cloud </div>
    <div class="article-body">CS6 und die Creative
        Cloud: Learn more about why this release is more
        than just a simple update and what exactly the
        Creative Cloud means.
    </div>
    <div class="article-footer">
        <img src="images/teaserMoreButton.png"
            width="110« height="24" />
    </div>
</article>
<article>...</article>
<div id="footer">
        (C) Insidrrr - offenes Kompetenznetzwerk f&uuml;r
        interaktive Medien
    </div>
</div>
</body>
</HTML>
```

3.3.1 Animating in Edge Animate

In Edge Animate, you simply open the HTML document with the Open dialog box. The page is displayed directly on the Stage, and the Elements panel on the right shows the document's entire DOM structure. You can select elements on the Stage and then animate them on the Timeline like any Edge Animate project.

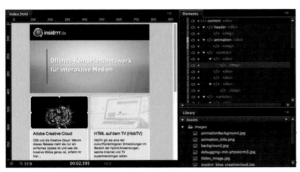

Figure 3.8
Edge Animate can open an existing HTML document for further editing without any additional steps

The final result can either be saved as usual or published in an optimized version (see chapter 6). Editing the HTML file in Edge Animate generates the necessary Edge Animate files in the same folder as the HTML document and links them to the header of the HTML document. In addition, CSS classes are also applied to all elements for animation. The entire animation logic is stored in external JavaScript files and applied to the document during runtime.

3.4 Basic Properties

Except for a few cases, changes to the basic properties of all assets are supported, thus making them context-independent.

3.4.1 Position, Size, and Opacity

The basic properties of position, size, and opacity can be modified for all asset types. Position is indicated by x and y coordinates in pixels (px). Basically, you can enter any coordinates for these properties, but only as whole numbers. Unlike Flash, CSS rules out the rendering of sub-pixels. See section 3.4.4 to learn more about how the composition behaves when extreme values are used that completely or partially position the element outside the Stage's viewable area.

The size for the element's width and height is also defined in pixels. If you want the ratio to always be maintained when minimizing or maximizing, you can enable the Link Width and Height option.

You can also use percentages instead of pixel values for flexible layouts. More on this topic can be found in section 3.9.4.

> ✎ **CSS Equivalent**
> The CSS properties being changed here are: left, top, transform, width, height and opacity. Here is one example of changing the position:
> ```
> style="left: 100px;
> transform:
> translateX(0);
> top: 20px;
> transform:
> translateY(0);"
> ```
>
> For width and height:
> ```
> style="width: 200px;
> height: 200px;"
> ```
>
> Opacity in CSS is handled as follows:
> ```
> style="opacity: 0.5;"
> ```

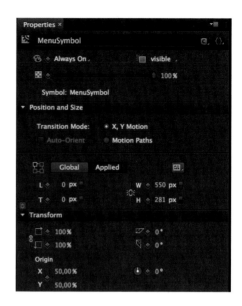

If you nest elements, such as dragging text element onto a DIV container on the Elements panel, you have the option to switch between Global and Applied (local) positioning. In this example, global positioning calculates the coordinates relative to the Stage. When you choose Applied, the coordinates displayed are relative to the parent container.

The third basic property, opacity, is used to change the transparency of an element. Here you can choose from 0% to 100% opacity with 0% being completely transparent.

Figure 3.9

Use opacity to change the transparency of an element

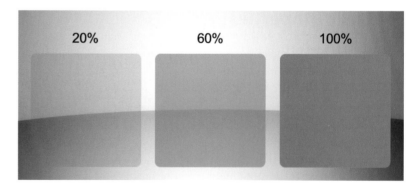

3.4.2 Changing Properties With Control Points

You can also change the properties of elements directly on the Stage rather than with the Property panel. If you select an item with the Selection tool, you can change the following properties with control points:

▶ • Position (x and y coordinates)

▶ • Size (width and height)

Figure 3.10
The Selection tool in action (default setting)

When you select an element with the Transform tool, you can modify the following additional properties directly on the Stage:

▶ Rotation and center of rotation

▶ Origin of transformation

▶ Rounded corners (only for shapes created in Edge Animate)

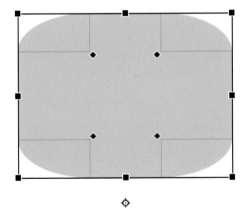

Figure 3.11
The Transform tool offers more options, such as making rounded corners

A third option is the Clipping tool. This tool lets you change the following properties of imported images:

▶ Container position (x and y coordinates)

▶ Container size (width and height)

▶ Image position (x and y coordinates)

▶ Image size (width and height)

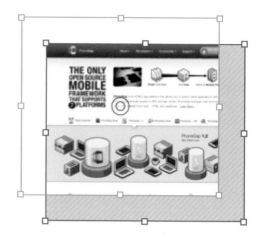

Figure 3.12

Use the Clipping tool to crop the display area of an image

3.4.3 Display Property

With extensive animations and applications, not all graphic elements are actually displayed at all times. Edge Animate uses the display property to control which elements are visible. This saves you the effort of manually moving inactive elements outside of the visible Stage area. All visual elements have this property, which itself has three states:

▶ always on

▶ on

▶ off

Timeline behavior when setting the display property for an element: The entire period for which an element is not displayed is shaded with a dark gray pattern. You cannot set another keyframe for this time period.

If you set the display property to *on* at a time later than 00:00, Edge Animate reacts by automatically setting the display for the preceding period to *off*. Each element is initially visible by default, so the setting would therefore have no effect. If the display of the element is changed over time through a keyframe and the display property is set to *always on*, all keyframes are removed from the Display lane in the Timeline after an error message. Keyframes already set for a specific period of time are not deleted when an element's display property is later deactivated. Rather, they remain visible in the Timeline and can be reactivated by moving them or turning the display property back on.

3.4.4 Overflow

HTML uses rectangles to contain any element on the Stage, even if the element does not appear as a rectangle because of its transparency. This bounding box is one indication of the rectangular layout. The bounding box is a frame that appears when an element has been selected to be transformed. Each element is represented in the background by a DIV container in HTML. This bounding box therefore indicates the exact dimensions of the DIV container. Since a DIV container can contain other elements, there are several display options for the child elements. (For more information on nesting elements, refer to section 3.5.) Normally, the elements contained in a DIV container are no larger than the container itself. In this case, you can simply ignore the Overflow option. However, if the elements are larger than the container, such as when you want to create a list with many elements and a scroll bar, you can change the container display and scroll properties with these four options:

> ▸ visible (default)
> ▸ hidden
> ▸ scroll
> ▸ auto

The default setting, *visible*, means that all overlapping content (in the negative coordinates) is displayed without any changes.

> **✎ CSS Equivalent**
> This Edge Animate method corresponds to the CSS display property. The *always on* setting means the display property does not change. While *on* sets the display property to block, the display of an element is hidden when *off* is selected and the value none is used.

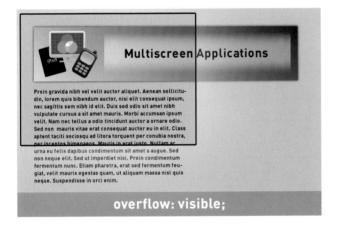

Figure 3.13
Set the Overflow option to *visible* so the entire content will be displayed, even when it goes outside of the container boundaries

Set the option to *hidden* and the excess content is simply cut off. Since scroll bars are never displayed here, a type of keyhole or masking effect is created. The contents of the container can still be modified and animated as needed. However, if you want to partially hide a single element, such as for a fade-in, it is better to do this through clipping (see section 3.4.8).

Figure 3.14

If the excess contents of a container can simply be cut off, *hidden* is the correct option to use

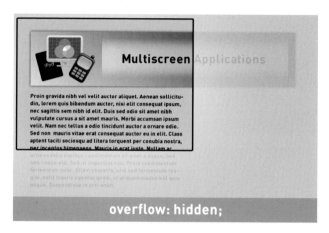

If you want to make the additional content accessible via scroll bars, set the option to *scroll*. However, this setting makes both horizontal and vertical scroll bars always visible even if they both are not needed, which is why this setting is rarely used.

Figure 3.15

For cases when you want both scroll bars, *scroll* is the correct setting

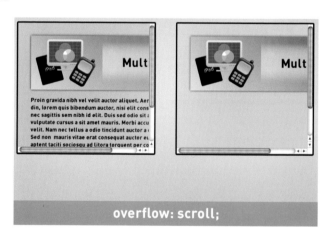

If you want to provide scroll bars to navigate through the content, *auto* is the right choice in most cases. As the name implies, scroll bars are displayed only when they are actually needed.

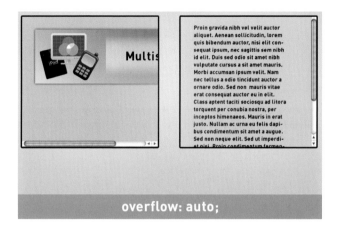

Figure 3.16
The *auto* setting means that scroll bars only appear when they are actually needed

Since the Stage itself is ultimately just a DIV container, you can manually set the overflow for the Stage, as well as for symbols. This is particularly important when other Edge Animate compositions or other HTML elements are involved, as is the case with a content management system. For such scenarios, the standard setting *visible* is not suitable.

3.4.5 Cursor

You can also set the appearance of the mouse cursor individually for all assets in your project. Simply select an element on the Stage and click the auto button on the Cursor section of the Property panel. A table with cursor icons from which you can choose a mouse cursor is displayed. You should always be careful when setting the cursor: for example, the pointer (hand icon) should be used for all clickable elements; the other cursors should only be used if they are really appropriate. Otherwise, they can be confusing to the user.

> ✎ **CSS Equivalent**
> This Edge Animate method corresponds to the CSS overflow property. For example, if you set the Overflow option to *auto*, the DOM will be changed as follows:
> `style="overflow: auto;"`

Figure 3.17
Edge Animate offers you many mouse cursors

3.4.6 Shadows

You can also define how shadows appear for all assets. Use the Shadow section in the Property panel to set the shadows. The button to the right of the Shadow section toggles the shadow on or off. Once you turn the shadow effect on, the previously grayed-out properties become active.

Figure 3.18

A small toggle switch in the Property panel turns on the shadow effect for individual elements

Shadows are used to create various spatial effects. There are two types of shadows available: drop shadows and inset shadows. The following image shows the four different shadows. Top left is a normal drop shadow. If you reduce the Blur value and increase the Spread value, you create a shadow with hard edges (top right). Setting the x and y coordinates to 0 creates an evenly distributed glow effect (bottom left). The last example shows a colored shadow. Not only can you set the color of a shadow, but also its opacity. These settings are made in the Color Picker dialog.

Figure 3.19

Different shadow options: outer shadows

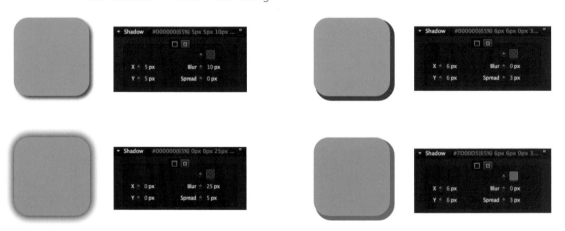

The inset shadow behaves in a similar manner. As the name suggests, the shadow is placed within (and does not go beyond the edges of) the shape. With the inset shadow, you can create pseudo-gradients that resemble a radial gradient, and give simple shapes a more 3-D look.

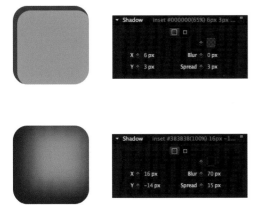

Figure 3.20
Different shadow options: inset shadows

An element can have only one shadow. However, you can freely combine both types of shadows, or several shadows of the same type. To do this, make both the color of the basic shape and the shadow transparent (not to be confused with the opacity of the entire element).

Figure 3.21
The opacity of the fill color can be changed in the Color Picker

In this way, you can overlap similar shapes so that the different shadows combine to create an interesting-looking object. The following example shows a colored shape with a slightly centered drop shadow. An inset shadow is laid on top, making the button appear three-dimensional. To create a more natural effect, the gray area is then covered with a slightly offset, pseudo-radial shadow to simulate a glow or a light source.

Figure 3.22
Combination of different shadows types

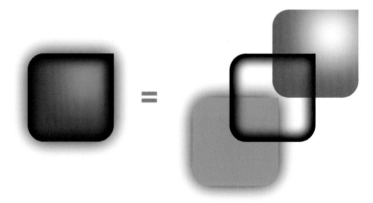

With a little tweaking, the shadow transitions can be made imperceptible so that a blur effect is created. If you would like to create special effects in a composition, such as spatial depth, you can design the background elements to create a depth of field. The following illustration shows how to achieve such an effect with three levels. Make sure that the drop shadow and inset shadow have the same gray level to create a smooth transition.

Figure 3.23
The combination of specific shadows
can simulate a blur

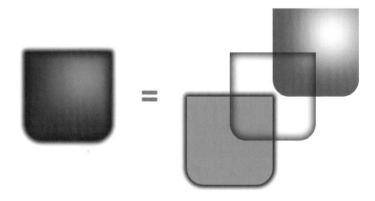

📑 **Project**
The files for this example can be downloaded from http://edgebuch. simonwidjaja.com
Project Name: Creation_Shadows

These different types of shadows are a simple way to enhance basic objects. The illustration shows a simple robot drawn in Edge Animate with rectangles, and a much livelier version on the right made with the use of simple shadows:

Figure 3.24
A simple character, embellished with shadows

This technique can also be used to create a complete scene with foreground and background. The following illustration is such a scene, consisting solely of basic shapes and shadows, without the use of any additional images. Of course, you should always keep an eye on browser performance with such experiments because scenes can become very complex and shadows need more computing power than flat surfaces. All shadow properties can be animated, but once they are set, shadow properties can no longer be changed on the Timeline.

Figure 3.25
The illustration depicts a scene that only consists of basic shapes with shadows

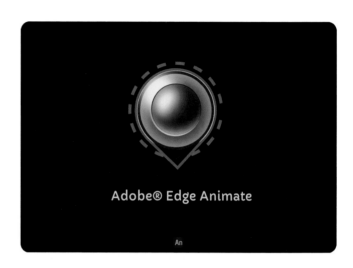

Figure 3.26
Another example of the creative use of
basic shapes with shadows

The project by Darrel Heath is another example of the use of basic shapes and shadows. The project's components are basic shapes created exclusively in Edge Animate that, when combined, depict a beautiful, interactive dial button (http://www.heathrowe.com/adobe-edge-animate-box-shadow-effects).

3.4.7 CSS Filters

One of the new features of Edge Animate version 1.5 is the integration of CSS filters. However, it should be noted that this is (still) not supported across all browsers. The small warning icon at the bottom right of the Stage provides information as soon as a CSS filter is applied. You should always keep an eye on this message when CSS filters are being used.

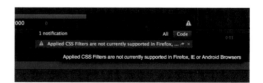

Thus, you should use CSS filters with caution, and at least for now, avoid them whenever possible.

CSS filters can be individually selected and used together in any combination. You can also animate them, as the diamond icon for keyframes indicates. In general, the following CSS filters are available:

Invert inverts the base color of the element. The percentage indicates the strength of the effect, where 100% produces the exact complementary color.

Hue-Rotate shifts the color of the element. The value indicates the degree of change, with 180° producing the complementary color and 360° producing the original color.

Contrast adjusts the color contrast.

Saturate allows you to adjust color saturation.

Sepia creates a yellowish-brown coloration. This creates an effect typical of old photographs.

Grayscale reduces the color to pure gray tones at 100%.

Blur creates a blur effect in which the element's pixels protrude out from the element.

Unlike Edge Animate's box-shadow property in the Shadow section (see section 3.4.6), the CSS shadow filter is a drop shadow, meaning it can only work on the outside of the element. Due to compatibility issues for the CSS filters described above, the box-shadow property should be used whenever possible.

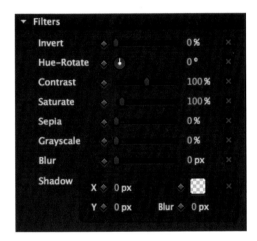

3.4.8 Clipping

All elements used in Edge Animate can be clipped. In most cases, this is only useful for images. If you want to clip an element, you first have to activate Clipping in the Clip section of the Property panel by clicking the button to the right of the Clip section to display the clip properties.

Once Clipping is active, you can set separate values for the left, top, right and bottom edges. All values are pixel values relative to the coordinate origin; in other words, the upper left corner of the element. These clip properties can be animated.

The following example shows an image that is clipped on the left and right, thus displaying only a partial area of the original image. When using Clipping, please avoid using unnecessarily large images in which some portions are never visible. Since images are completely loaded into the browser whether or not they are displayed in their entirety, large, clipped images produce unnecessarily large project files.

> ✎ **Clipping**
>
> Clipping should only be used for animations and not for the cropping of images. If the cropped parts of the image will never be seen outside of the clipping mask, the images should first be properly cropped in Photoshop to avoid adding unnecessary image data to the project.

3.4.9 Gradients

Starting with the release of Edge Animate 1.5, it is possible to create gradients in addition to the normal selection of colors. These are implemented through the Background Image option to the right of the familiar Color Picker. The gradient levels are based on the actual color. With this feature, transparencies can be used to achieve very interesting effects.

Basically, if you opt to use a gradient, you have the choice between linear and radial gradients. For linear gradients, you can set the direction of the gradient with the gradient angle degree. For radial gradients, you can change the X and Y coordinates to move the origin of the gradient. The Color Stop bar on the left is used to set the relationship between the colors and their sequence in the gradient. You can add more color stops just by clicking. They can be deleted by pulling them away from the Color Stop bar to the right or the left. As usual, set the color for each color stop with the Color Picker, and the transparency in the alpha channel.

The Repeating option sets the selected gradient to repeat the color stops consecutively, as in tiling.

The gradient can be saved as a preset to use again on other elements. The small diamond keyframe icon next to the Gradient option indicates that these can be animated in the usual manner.

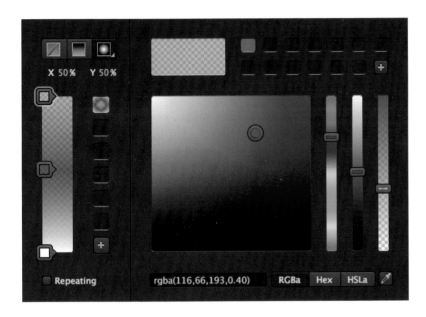

3.5 Nesting and Symbols

As with almost all visual design and authoring tools, Edge Animate offers you various ways to combine multiple items into groups. You can nest elements as a way to group them, or transform a group of elements into a symbol.

The grouping of elements is useful when you want to move the elements all at once or animate them. To create a group, you have two options. The first option is simply dragging elements to another layer in the Elements panel to create a group hierarchy. Although you can nest any elements together, the target lane must be a container or a DIV element. Text and graphics cannot have child elements.

Figure 3.27

Grouping layers in the Elements panel

As a second option, you can also combine multiple objects on the Stage by accessing a context menu with a right click and choosing Group Elements in DIV to create a new group. Unlike the first option, this creates a new container. Now you can animate this new container and any child elements as if it were a single element. Grouped elements can be ungrouped by accessing a context menu with a right-click and choosing Ungroup Elements. Both functions can also be accessed under the main Modify menu.

On the other hand, if you convert one or more elements into a symbol, the various components or elements contained in the symbol are encapsulated and can no longer be directly selected on the Stage. The symbol now appears as a single layer in the Elements panel. The individual components of the symbol will only be displayed in the Elements panel by double clicking on the symbol. This can be useful for very complex object combinations.

Figure 3.28
Grouping elements through a right-click context menu

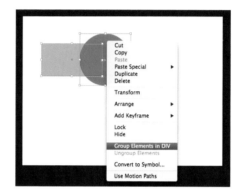

There are two other advantages of symbols. On one hand, each symbol has its own Timeline separate from the Stage that can be started and stopped independently. This means it is easy to create asynchronous animations and interactivity. More on this topic can be found in section 4.5.2.

Figure 3.29
A symbol can also be used for grouping elements

The second advantage is that symbols can be reused. Once you create a symbol, it is listed in the Library panel under the Symbols section. A symbol definition in the Library is a blueprint for your group of objects that you can reuse in your project as often as needed. For example, you can create page templates or frequent animation sequences that you can edit globally. Since you can program the placement of symbols with actions, a symbol definition is still maintained in the Library even if you have removed all instances of it from the Stage.

All instances of a symbol are based on the same blueprint, meaning they are initially identical. Like with all other elements, use the Property panel to change the symbol instance's properties at a later point. Thus, the symbol definition is the lowest common denominator. Section 5.8.1 on buttons will show you how to insert dynamic content initially created on the instance level into a symbol definition through the use of code.

3.6 Exporting and Reusing Symbols

Since symbols are often used as templates, Edge Animate offers the ability to export all symbol definitions for easy application in other projects. To export a symbol, right-click on it in the Library panel and choose Export.

Figure 3.30
Symbols can be exported from the Library for reuse

For exported symbols, Edge Animate uses the native file format *.ansym. The file format is actually just a ZIP archive containing the necessary HTML and JavaScript files. If you rename the file, you can unpack the archive and view the contents of the symbol.

You can load exported symbol definitions into any Edge Animate composition by clicking on the plus button in the Symbol section of the Library panel and then choosing Import Symbols. The selected symbol and all its data is loaded and embedded in the current project. There is no difference between self-created and imported symbols; both can be modified in any manner. The external symbol file is no longer needed after the import, and can be deleted.

In this way, you can create large collections of symbols that can be reused in any project and shared with other web designers.

Figure 3.31

Any available symbols can be imported into the Library

3.6.1 Templates

Edge Animate CC's templates are another way to exchange and build ready-made composition templates, which are then loaded into a gallery, stored, and reused for multiple purposes. This feature allows you to build Edge Animate compositions according to the same structure or a specific basic layout. This modularity avoids the constant or repetitive work of building similar compositions from scratch.

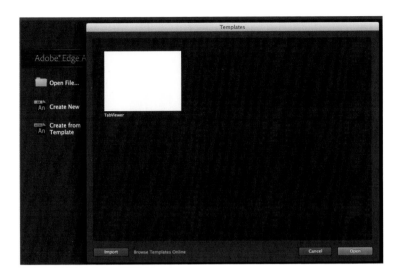

Templates can store images, text, symbols, fonts, and any individual modifications you make to a composition. The creation of a template produces an .antmpl file that can be easily extracted from the basic file structure and sent to other users.

Name   TabViewer.antmpl
Kind   Adobe Edge Animate Template File
Size   81 KB
Created   Dienstag, 11. Juni 2013 18:10
Modified   Dienstag, 11. Juni 2013 18:10
Last opened   Dienstag, 11. Juni 2013 18:10

A composition based on a template can be created either by selecting the option on the Getting Started panel or via File > Create From Template.

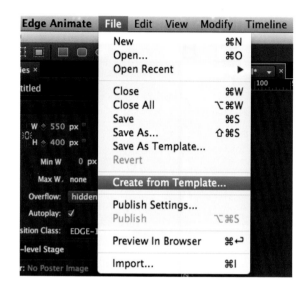

Templates can also be easily created by saving any composition as a template with the File menu command, Save As Template. The new template will appear in the list of available templates when you select Create From Template.

3.7 Additional Element Properties

In addition to the standard properties for all asset types, the different element types have their own specific properties.

3.7.1 Stage

The Stage offers additional properties for Down-level compatibility and Pre-loader behavior; text elements offer many typeface properties, and shapes have settings for controlling the fill color and borders.

Figure 3.32
Property panel with Stage section settings

3.7.2 Basic Shapes

As soon as you choose one of the basic shapes, the Property panel changes to display specific settings. In addition to the standard properties, you can now also define aspects such as rounded corners.

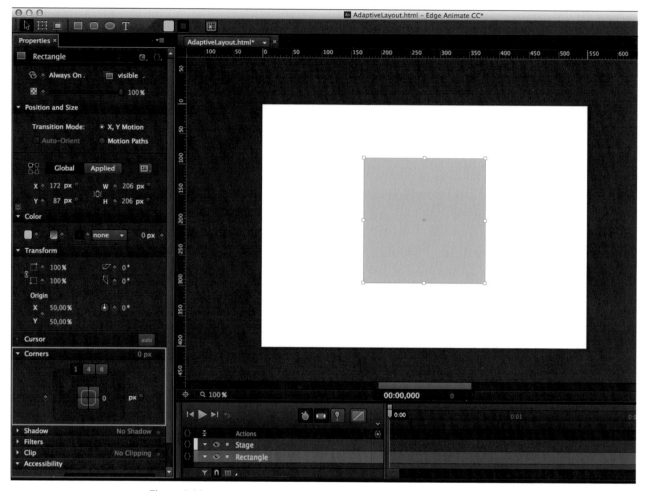

Figure 3.33

Property panel with settings
for basic shapes

3.7.3 Text

For text elements, the Property panel provides all relevant text-formatting properties such as font, font weight, and text alignment. The double arrow button in the lower left corner in the Text section (circled in the figure here) also displays settings for letter spacing, word spacing, line spacing, and indentation of the first line.

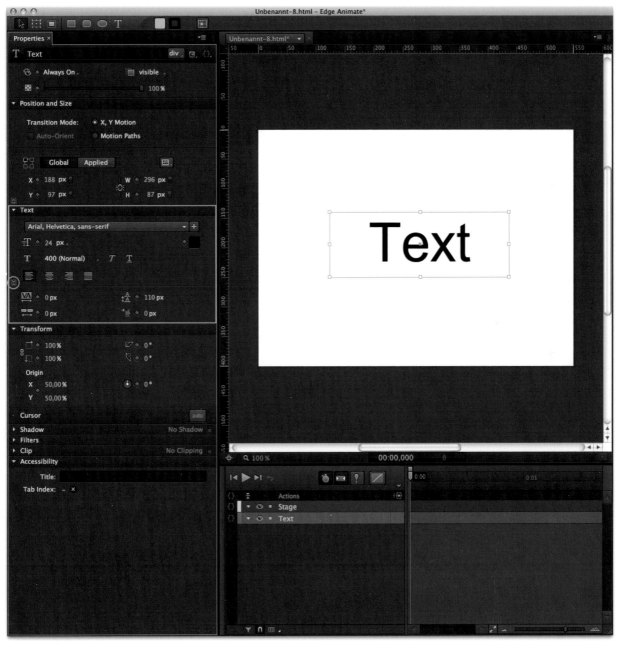

Figure 3.34
Property panel with Text section settings

3.7.4 Image

When an image is selected, you have access to an additional Image section on the Property panel that lets you swap out an already-linked image and set the coordinates and dimensions for the background image (CSS property `back-ground-image`). If the IMG tag is selected rather than the default DIV container tag, you can also set the Alt text for the image in this section.

Figure 3.35

Property panel with Image section settings

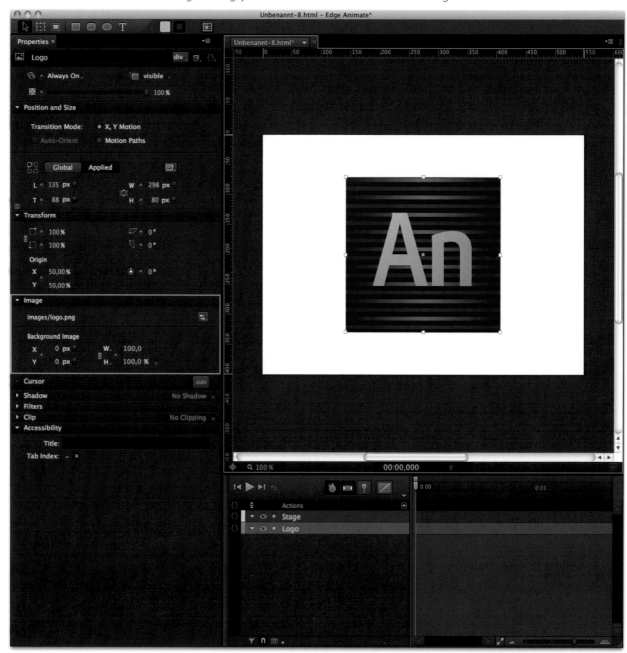

3.7.5 Symbol

Besides standard properties for symbols, the Property panel also contains a checkbox for turning scrubbing on and off in the Playback section. When enabled, you can scrub the playhead on the Timeline, and the playhead for the symbol will also be moved. When this option is unchecked, the symbols do not change in the Stage preview. However, this switch does not affect the behavior of symbols at runtime.

Figure 3.36

Property panel with Playback section settings for symbols

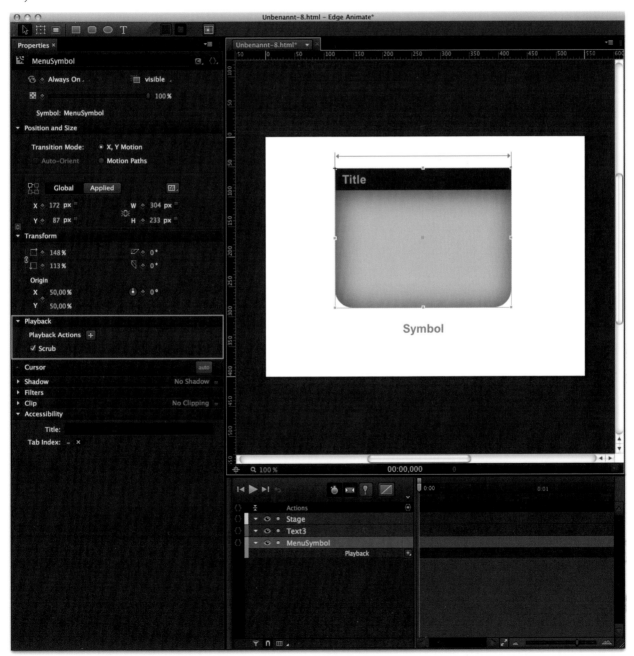

3.8 Custom Fonts

Gone are the days when you had to depict custom fonts as images or with Flash. For a long time now, many other fonts besides just Verdana or Arial have been available as a design tool. Since the various browsers behave differently with custom fonts, creating websites with non-standard fonts is not necessarily a simple matter. But the web would not be the web if it did not offer different solutions for this issue. There are already several font services that offer various font pools with embed codes for easy integration into your website. This embed code loads your selected font when your website is called and adjusts the font display based on the browser in use. This spares you the hassle of dealing with the quirks between different browsers, and instead simply uses the fonts as in any other program.

I would like to introduce two very popular resources for custom fonts: Google Fonts and Adobe Typekit.

3.8.1 Google Fonts

The search engine giant offers more than 500 web fonts at www.google.com/webfonts. All fonts are available under an open source license, meaning their use for both personal and commercial projects is entirely free of charge. Since mid-2012, Google Fonts is also available in the Google Drive application (formerly Google Docs). The service's website offers a highly intuitive user interface that makes it easy to search the entire font pool. In addition to numerous filter functions, there is even a review function that lets you compare the different selected fonts.

Figure 3.37
The Google Fonts service offers many free fonts that are easy to load into Edge Animate

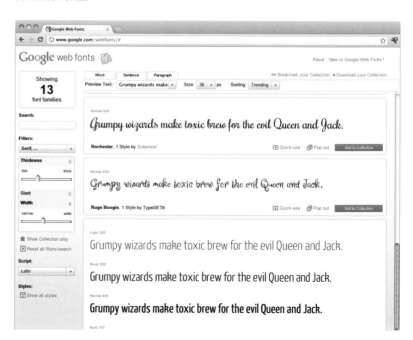

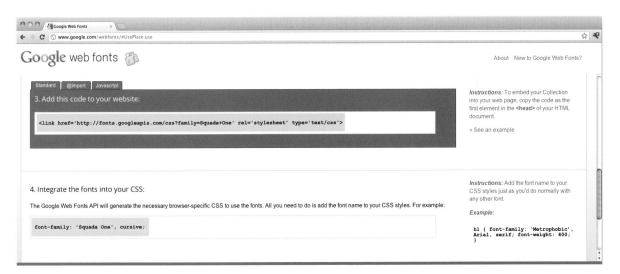

Figure 3.38

To embed the fonts, you will need the embed code and the name of the font (both are highlighted in red)

The integration is very simple. After you determine what font styles (e.g., regular, bold, italic, etc.) and character sets (e.g. Latin) you will need, Google Fonts provides a one-line code to embed in your own page in HTML. How Edge Animate handles this process is explained in section 3.8.3.

The biggest advantage here is certainly the open source licensing that eliminates a lengthy login process—a great perk for anyone wanting to experiment with various fonts without having to register. However, the licensing model is also the only significant disadvantage because you will not find any commercial fonts, which are often stipulated by corporate design guidelines, here.

If you are you interested in open source fonts, I recommend the following blog about Google Fonts: http://googlewebfonts.blogspot.de

3.8.2 Adobe Typekit

Adobe Typekit (www.typekit.com) is a font service that provides fonts for websites. Unlike Google Fonts, Typekit is a paid premium service that offers an extensive library of high-quality, copyrighted fonts. The cost of selecting and using Typekit fonts is based on how many websites (domains) use the fonts and the estimated number of page views per month. However, there is a free trial rate, which offers you the chance to use two fonts from a limited font pool for a single website. The trial offer limits the monthly number of page views to 25,000 and automatically displays a small Typekit badge at the bottom left corner of the website. If you want to avoid these restrictions, you can select from different plans starting at $24.99 per year.

Figure 3.39

Something for everyone: Typekit offers everything from a free trial plan to the all-inclusive business plan

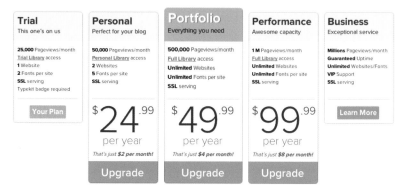

Figure 3.40

In addition to free fonts, Adobe Typekit offers numerous professional fonts

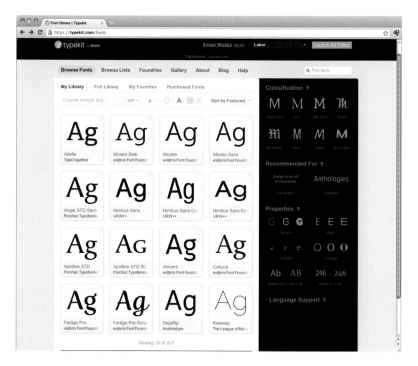

This is especially advantageous for business projects where compliance with corporate style guides is essential, because you are not necessarily limited to the fonts offered on Typekit. You can also purchase professional fonts from one of several providers, such as FontShop (www.fontshop.com), and then have it hosted on Typekit. FontShop makes this process a snap since the two font services work closely together. The Fontshop font is automatically sent to Typekit during the ordering process, making it unnecessary to download and set up the font on Typekit.

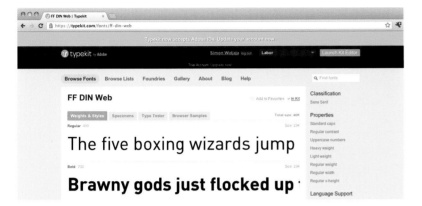

Figure 3.41
You can even use Typekit to set up professional fonts from third-party companies such as FontShop

Typekit also offers features, such as filtering and sorting according to font classification (Sans Serif, Serif, Script, Mono, Hand) and various other properties, such as weight, width, or small caps, for browsing its font pool. Once you have decided on one or more fonts, you can add them to the Kit Editor.

Load the font, and choose Launch Kit Editor on the menu to start the program. The editor gives you the code to embed in your HTML page in addition to various CSS selectors. The following section will explain more deeply how this process is handled in Edge Animate.

Problems Loading the Font?

Typekit was acquired by Adobe in late 2011 and is gradually being integrated into Adobe products. Typekit will likely be directly integrated into later versions of Edge Animate.

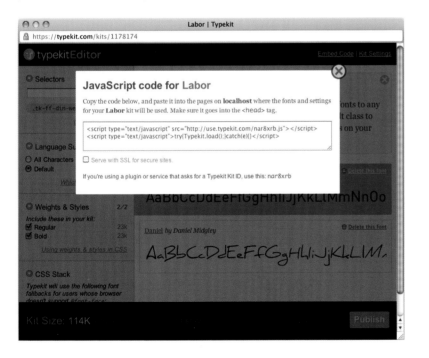

Figure 3.42
The Kit Editor in Typekit also gives you the embed code for linking your selected fonts

3.8.3 Embedding Fonts in Edge Animate

Let us look at how to integrate the selected fonts into your Edge Animate project. We will use two fonts from the pool of Google Fonts as a starting point: Dosis and Bad Script.

The two embed code are as follows:

```
<link href='http://fonts.googleapis.com/
css?family=Dosis' rel='stylesheet' type='text/css'>

<link href='http://fonts.googleapis.com/
css?family=Bad+Script' rel='stylesheet' type='text/
css'>
```

The font families in the CSS appear as follows:

```
font-family: 'Dosis', sans-serif;
font-family: 'Bad Script', cursive;
```

Once you have this information, you can add the fonts to Edge Animate in the Fonts section on the Library panel by clicking the + icon on the right. In the dialog, first indicate the Font Fallback List with the font names. This Fallback List ensures that a suitable font is selected as an alternative in case the primary font cannot be used for any reason (e.g., not supported by the browser, download error). Next, add the embed code for each font and save the settings.

> ✎ **Problems Loading the Font?**
>
> If you have problems with loading custom fonts, first check your firewall settings. These often prevent loading font information from Edge Animate.

Figure 3.43
Custom fonts can be added using an embed code

Repeat the procedure for the second font. Even though font services such as Google Fonts can combine multiple fonts in an embed code, the first version of Edge Animate requires you to add the fonts separately.

Once the fonts have been added, they appear in the Property panel along with the other fonts and can be assigned to any text elements.

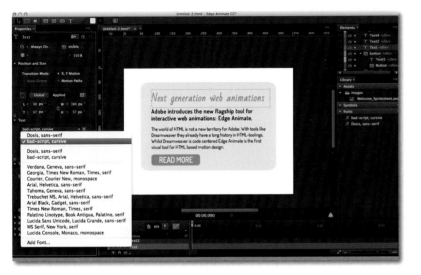

Figure 3.44
Like any other fonts, custom fonts can
be applied via the Text section of the
Property panel

When dealing with fonts, you have to keep in mind that not all browsers
support all font options in the same way. For example, text shadows are not
supported in Internet Explorer 8 or 9.

3.9 Flexible Layouts

Ever since the proliferation of web-enabled smartphones and tablets, web and
app designers are now confronted with the necessity of creating layouts that fit
a variety of different screen sizes and resolutions. Those designers still creating
layouts for a specific resolution, such as 800 x 600 pixels or 1024 x 768 pixels, run
the risk of angering or simply not reaching a significant portion of their target
audience. To that end, different concepts have been developed to address these
problems and offer solutions. The current buzz is about responsive or adaptive
design, which means that a given website or app should be able to automatically adapt to the display capabilities of different devices (desktop, netbook, tablet,
smartphone or Smart TV) without requiring the user to intervene. Some large
companies such as Google are already devoting a lot of attention to mobile
devices and designing their user interfaces under the principle Mobile First.

A thorough responsive design ensures that devices only load the kind of data
that they actually require, e.g., images in the right resolution and fonts they can
interpret. This is done through media queries. Unfortunately, the first version of
Edge Animate does not yet offer this infrastructure, which is why Adobe uses
flexible layouts rather than responsiveness. This capability will certainly be added in subsequent versions.

Let's look again at how to create flexible layout compositions with Edge Animate that can then be optimally displayed on small and large devices without
any problems. In sample project 3.10.1, we will look at an actual case study.

Project
The files for this example can be
downloaded from http://edgebuch.
simonwidjaja.com
Project Name: Creation_Fonts

3.9.1 Relative Values (Percentages)

Flexibility in layouts always starts by avoiding fixed values or pixel values. A composition whose Stage is 600 px wide will always be displayed in this width, although some mobile browsers simply scale down the entire content of a page to fit the width of the device. However, this method is not part of responsive layout and is far from ideal. Text is often barely readable and buttons are hard to distinguish, let alone use. To make an existing layout flexible, you have to change fixed pixel values of relative percentages. Edge Animate offers this option for almost all properties that are defined in pixels (by default). These include width, height, x and y coordinates, rounded corners and the font size.

In Edge Animate, the percentage size and position information always refer to the parent container, namely the Stage itself or the symbol that contains the corresponding elements. In most cases, the Stage is the primary element on which all the other elements are organized. To make the Stage flexible, you simply need to change the width and/or height of the Stage to percentages by using the small unit toggles next to the size properties.

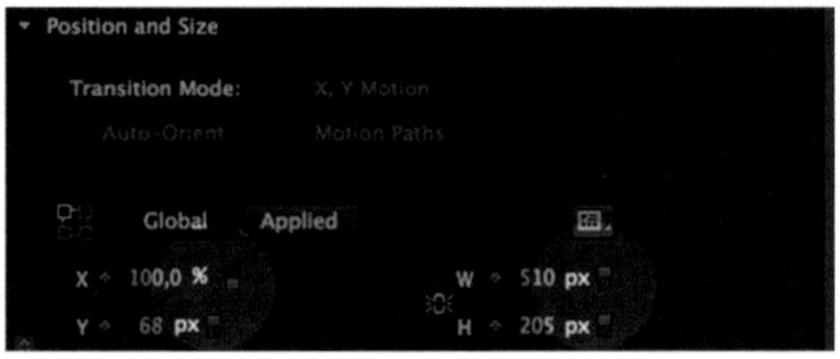

Figure 3.45

The unit toggle can switch between absolute and relative values

As soon as you change the Stage width or height to percentages, sliders appear on the vertical and/or horizontal rulers with which you can simulate a preview for the various resolutions directly in Edge Animate.

Figure 3.46

The sliders on the rulers can simulate various layout widths and heights directly in Edge Animate

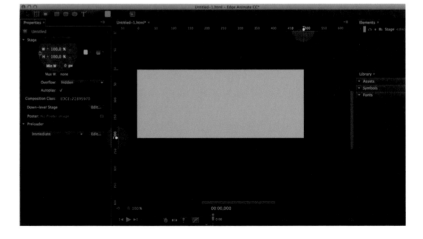

3.9.2 Minimum and Maximum Width

In most cases, it helps to set a minimum and maximum width. You can apply these settings to the stage itself and also to each symbol individually. In the example below, such settings would automatically adjust the composition to the width of the browser window, but no smaller than 600 px and no larger than 1200 px. However, the height always has a fixed value of 200 px. Make sure that the Overflow option is set to *hidden* to prevent elements from unexpectedly showing outside of their container edges.

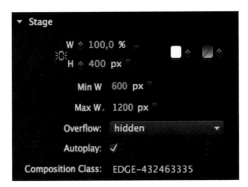

Figure 3.47
A Stage with a flexible width, as well as a minimum and maximum width, has an optimal display on different devices

3.9.3 Arranging Elements Flexibly

Of course, in many cases it is not enough just to use percentages for coordinate or size properties. Say, for example, you want an element to always align with the right side of a composition. These settings are no longer sufficient. To achieve such positioning, the Position and Size section on the Property panel contains an icon with four small squares for relative positioning. For example, choose the Relative to Bottom and Right square on the icon and the element will always maintain its current distance from the bottom and right edges when the Stage changes in size.

Figure 3.48
Figure 3.48
In Edge Animate, elements may also be
aligned to the right or lower edge of the
Stage

The following example shows how to fill a flexible Stage with shapes that
each take up 50% of the total Stage area. The right section always has the same
dimensions as the left, but is aligned to the right edge of the Stage.

Figure 3.49
An example of a flexible layout with
sections sized relative to the Stage

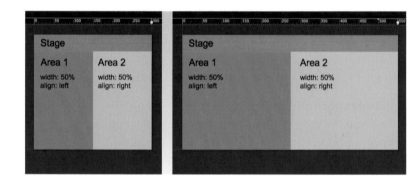

3.9.4 Presets for Flexible Layouts

In many cases, you have to combine the various layout options. It helps to be
familiar with the many CSS properties in order to keep track of everything. However, to maintain a certain level of intuitiveness, Edge Animate offers standard
settings (presets) that simplify some of the more unusual layout combinations.
These presets can be accessed via the Layout Preset button in the Position and
Size section of the Property panel. The left side of the Layout Presets dialog
displays the various presets. The right side displays which CSS properties are
affected and modified by the particular preset.

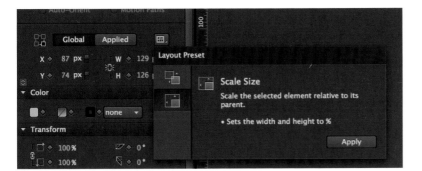

Figure 3.50
Edge Animate offers you many layout presets

While only two presets for positioning and size are available for basic shapes, the preset list for specific image elements is considerably larger. You also have various options for positioning and scaling the actual image in its container.

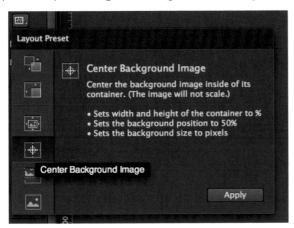

Figure 3.51
Layout presets for images are a bit more versatile

The above example shows the Center Background Image preset. Here the width and height of the container are changed to percentage values, the background position is set to 50%, and the background size is set in pixels. This results in the background image never being scaled or distorted. Rather, only the displayed section is adjusted (keyhole effect). The sample project in section 3.10.1 will show you how to apply this effect in a specific project.

Anyone wanting to go beyond flexible layouts and create independent layouts for different stage sizes must either manually edit the code or use an available extension. Section 3.10.2 will introduce you to one of those extensions.

3.10 Lessons

Now that you have learned about the theory, the following examples will show you how flexible layouts are used. First, we will create a flexible banner with Edge Animate's native tools. Then we will look at the Edge Commons extension to create different layouts for different sizes.

3.10.1 Flexible Banners for Different Resolutions

📖 Project

The files for this example can be downloaded from http://edgebuch. simonwidjaja.com
Project Name:
Creation_FlexibleLayout

In this step-by-step sample project, we will create a simple banner with a flexible layout so that its content will display well in various resolutions, from smartphones to desktop monitors. All text must always be visible and not scaled. The finished banner can then be integrated into any website.

The banner should only be flexible in its width. The height should be fixed, as is usually the case in actual projects. We will define the minimum width as 600 px and the maximum width as 1200 px. The result should look as follows:

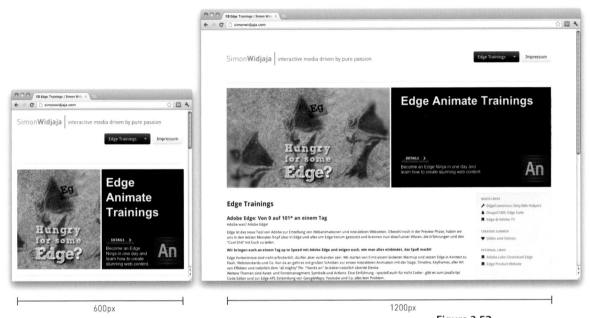

Figure 3.52

The flexible composition in different screen sizes

1. Graphics • First, we create artwork in any graphics program. The graphics for the sample project were created with Adobe Photoshop and saved as a PNG file.

2. New project • We create a new project in Edge Animate with the height set to 350 px. First we set the width to 1200 px. Next, we set the minimum width to 600 px, as per the project requirements, and the maximum width to 1200 px.

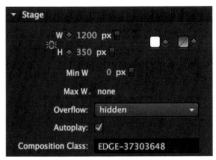

3. Static layout · Now we drag all the graphics onto the Stage and into their designated places. We also create the text in Edge Animate so that we can make its width flexible.

4. Flexible Stage · To adjust the width of the Stage to the width defined in the HTML document and the browser window, use the unit toggle next to the width property to switch to percentages. Next, make sure that the Overflow option is set to *hidden* so that all elements outside the Stage are invisible. Now we can use the preview slider on the top ruler to simulate different widths for our composition. Since we have not yet defined the behavior of the individual elements, we see no differences when changing the display size. Before setting the layout behavior for the individual elements, we return the preview slider back to 1200 px so that all settings are based on this default value.

5. Right-edge aligned logo · For the Animate logo, we set the alignment to Relative to Top and Right in the Position and Size section of the Property panel. Thus, we have made our first setting for flexible behavior, which we can see as soon as we move the preview slider.

6. Right side · Now we select all other elements on the right side except the logo and change the x-coordinate from pixels to percentages.

    When we now change the width with the preview slider, we see that the positions of those elements are recalculated. Lastly, besides the position of the two text elements, we also need to ensure that all elements adjust to the width of the available area. To do this, we set the width of both elements to percentages. However, before you complete the final step, you must first move the preview slider back to 1200 px to restore the default width, otherwise the calculations will be off. The right side is now finished. We can move the preview slider anywhere between the two minimum and maximum sizes without obscuring any content on the right side. Only the image on the left side is not correctly displayed as we approach the minimum width.

7. Left side · In order for the slogan on the left to always be completely visible, we must ensure that the image container fits in the width and that the image content is always centered. To do this, we first set the preview slider back to our standard width of 1200 px, and then switch the image width to percentages. In addition, we also apply the layout preset Center Background Image so that the slogan is always displayed in the middle.

8. Final result · The flexible banner is now ready and can be opened in the browser. Depending on how it will be used, the project can now be exported as an optimized web version or for digital publications. You will learn more about this in section 6.3.3.

3.10.2 Independent Layouts for Different Screen Sizes

Of course, the flexible layout described above has one serious disadvantage—it can only display very limited content. It must be possible to display the tiniest details of all content in percentages. Often it is necessary or more practical to create independent layouts for different screen sizes that adjust to defined widths. The first version of Edge Animate does not yet directly support this feature unless you program the code using the Edge Animate API. Since such functionality is needed quite often, a few colleagues and I have developed a free extension for Edge Animate that offers a very simple way to create independent layouts, in addition to numerous other features: *Edge Commons—Dirty Little Helpers for Edge Animate*. For more information about Edge Commons, refer to section 7.4.

In the following example, we will use the Adaptive Layouts feature from the Edge Commons Library to generate three independent layouts. The following screenshots show the layout for screen widths of 400-599 px, 600-799 px and > 800 px.

Project
The files for this example can be downloaded from http://edgebuch.simonwidjaja.com
Project Name:
Creation_AdaptiveLayouts

Figure 3.53

Independent layouts for different sizes with Edge Commons

1. Stage and containers • First, we create a new project and set the width of the Stage to percentages to give our composition a flexible width. Now we need a container that will contain the layouts to be created. We draw a new rectangle across the entire area of the Stage and name it "adaptiveContainer."

2. Different layouts · Now let's look at the actual layouts. We draw another rect-
    angle, this time with the dimensions of the specific target layout. It is best to
    start with the biggest one, so this rectangle will have a dimension of 350 x
    1200 pixels. Since we will let Edge Commons handle the positioning of each
    layout later on, we must save the layouts as symbols in the Library so that
    they can automatically be generated at runtime. To do this, we change the
    rectangle you just created into a symbol. Double-click the symbol to display
    the layout. We can now place our texts and graphics. Since a symbol offers
    us an additional Timeline separate from the Stage Timeline, we can also
    create animations within the symbol. Once you are done with the layout,
    you can click out of it and return to the Stage. The symbol can now be safely
    deleted from the Stage since it is retained in the Library. Repeat this process
    for all layouts. In this example, you should create three symbols with the
    following widths: 400 px, 600 px and 800 px.

3. Naming symbols · Since Edge Commons automatically places the symbol
    on the Stage according to the current browser width, you have to give the
    symbols unique names that are recognized by Edge Commons. Rename
    the symbols as follows: layout + the width of each layout. In our case, the
    symbol names are layout400, layout600 and layout800.

4. Download Edge Commons · The creation of the layout is now complete, so
    let's work on the extension. Edge Commons must be loaded when the com-
    position is loaded in the browser so that the right layout can be displayed
    immediately. This can be done by either using the online version of Edge
    Commons or using the download version and saving it in the project folder.
    In this example we will use the latter and save the Edge Commons 0.5.0.js
    file in the /libs directory.

5. Add creationComplete action • The extension is still not active. We add a creationComplete action, which is executed as soon as the composition is fully loaded.

Figure 3.54
The Edge Commons extension is loaded on the creationComplete event

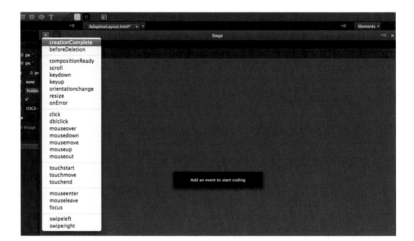

6. Running the script · To activate, we use the built-in Edge Animate function `yepnope()` to reload the extension. With the following code, we not only load the extension, but also activate our adaptive layouts with the function `EC.setAdaptiveLayouts(...)`:

```
yepnope({
   load: "http://cdn.edgecommons.org/an/1.0.0/js/min/
   EdgeCommons.js",
   complete: function() {
      EC.setAdaptiveLayouts (
         [400, 600, 800], sym, "adaptiveContainer"
   );
 }
});
```

7. Result · The adaptive layout is now ready and can b e opened in the browser. When the browser is minimized or maximized, the layout jumps up or down to the defined markers. If the composition is loaded into a smaller width, the corresponding layout is immediately loaded. The latter is especially necessary for mobile devices.

> ✎ **EC.setAdaptiveLayouts()**
> The Edge Commons function `EC.setAdaptiveLayouts()` expects three arguments. The first argument is a list (array) of widths for the layouts being used. The second argument is always a reference to the current symbol (sym). The third argument is the name of the layout container. The number of different layouts is flexible and can be adapted to the existing layout.

4

Animation

4   Animation

Now that you know the most important features and techniques of creation, this chapter will teach you how to create animations with the Timeline, the Pin and keyframes.

4.1   The Timeline

While Edge Animate's Stage displays the spatial layout of the individual graphic elements, the Timeline shows you the change of the different properties over a defined period of time. To do this, you play what Adobe calls the Timeline.

4.1.1   Keyframes

On the Timeline, keyframes are used to link different states of elements to certain points in time. If not explicitly deactivated, the transitions of individual images between the keyframes are automatically interpolated in a process known as tweening. For example, if you animate an element on the x-axis with two keyframes from 100 px to 200 px, the intermediate steps are automatically generated. Basically, you can animate almost all properties with keyframes in Edge Animate except for font weight, text alignment, and how the mouse cursor is displayed. Keyframes can be added to the Timeline through a number of different methods:

Setting keyframes in the Property panel • To set the value of a property such as a coordinate, the font size, or the fill color for a specific point in time, drag the playhead to where you want the property to take effect. Click the small diamond icon (see image) next to the property. Now you have set a keyframe, which appears as a white diamond on the Timeline. If the property does not yet have a keyframe, a new lane for the property is added. However, if the lane already exists, the keyframe is added to the lane.

Figure 4.1

Setting keyframes with the diamond icon in the Property panel

Setting keyframes on the Timeline in lanes · Once an animation lane for a property exists, more keyframes can be added directly into the Timeline. Again, you do this by using the small diamond icon to the right of the corresponding property.

Figure 4.2

Setting keyframes on the Timeline in lanes

Automatically setting keyframes · Frequently, animation sequences are created in their actual order. Edge Animate uses the Auto-Keyframe Mode to do this. This mode is activated by default and automatically sets keyframes when an element is moved or a property is changed. However, this mode is only active if an animation lane already exists for the property in question, or if at least one keyframe has already been set. In this way, you can move new elements to a specific position without creating any unwanted keyframes. Animations can be created very quickly in this mode, but you must always make changes carefully in order to not create unwanted animation sequences. The Auto-Transition Mode is a special case. This option is rarely deactivated in a regular workflow. However, if you want to set the properties directly (in other words, switch off the automatic calculation of the transitions between two states), you need to deactivate Auto-Transition Mode. An example scenario for this mode is a sprite sheet animation (flip book effect), in which part of an image changes in a fast tempo without the image itself visibly moving over a long period of time (see the sample project in section 4.5.4).

Figure 4.3

(1) Auto-Keyframe Mode

(2) Auto-Transition Mode

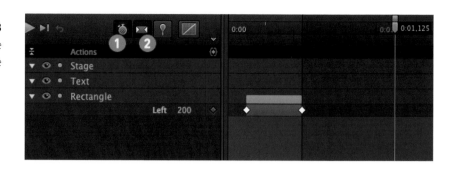

Setting keyframes with the Pin • The Pin is a second imaginary playhead that makes it easy to create an animation between two points in the Timeline. Whenever you want to animate up to or after a point in time, the Pin is the right tool. There are three ways to activate it. Firstly, the Timeline menu contains a Toggle Pin command for activating the Pin.

You can also enable or disable the Pin by double-clicking the main playhead, or by toggling it on and off with the P key on your keyboard. Be sure to turn off the Pin after creating the animation, otherwise you will accidentally create unwanted keyframes. The figures below illustrate how to use the Pin.

▸ (1) shows the normal mode with the Pin turned off.

▸ Once the Pin is turned on (2), a small blue pin appears directly above the yellow playhead.

▸ Now the Pin can be moved anywhere on the Timeline (3). A shaded band with arrows becomes visible. The bar in this example is blue because the Pin is behind the actual playhead.

▸ If you move an element or change its properties, the values are set at the point on the Timeline where the red line and yellow playhead are positioned. The initial state is pinned down where the Pin is located, adding a transition in between the two states (4).

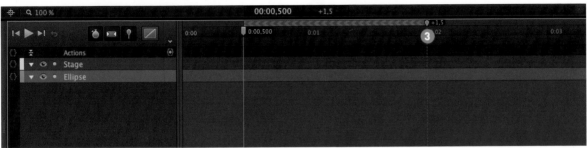

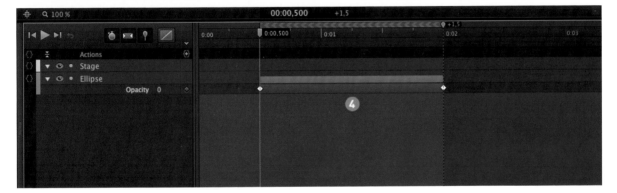

The Pin can also be placed before the main playhead. In this case, the directional band is displayed in yellow. When the Pin is located behind the playhead with a blue directional band, we are creating an animation from the newly-set state back to the original state. Animation with a yellow directional band animates in the opposite direction: from the initial state towards the new state.

Figure 4.4

The Pin is a second imaginary playhead that greatly simplifies creating animation between two points in time

Figure 4.5

If the Pin is set before the playhead, the animation direction is reversed

4.1.2 Other Timeline Functions

The Timeline offers other functions that enable improved accuracy in complex compositions and the creation of elaborate animation sequences:

Figure 4.6

The Timeline in Edge Animate offers numerous additional functions, such as filtering animated lanes, or the grid

- ▸ Expand/Collapse Lanes: This function lets you temporarily hide animation lanes so that only the main element levels are displayed.
- ▸ Filtering: A small filter icon is located on the bottom left of the Timeline for temporarily hiding any lanes that are not yet animated or that do not have keyframes.
- ▸ Timeline Snapping: The magnet icon next to the filter icon controls Timeline Snapping and is activated by default. The playhead snaps onto existing keyframes when Timeline Snapping is activated.
- ▸ Grid / Grid Size: This option shows/hides a grid within the Timeline, which is helpful for complex animations. To activate the grid, simply click the small, three-column grid icon. You can change the grid spacing with the white arrow next to it. A menu appears, offering several presets in seconds or fps (frames per second). The snapping feature also applies to the grid.
- ▸ Zoom: The zoom slider for changing the size of the currently displayed Timeline is in the lower right corner of the Timeline. To the left is a double arrow button: Zoom Timeline to Fit. This button automatically sets the zoom level of the view of the Timeline to a state that shows the actual length of the animation.

4.1.3 Playback

If you have created your first animations with keyframes, you can directly view them within Edge Animate. Use the Play button in the upper left corner of the Timeline, or press the spacebar to play the animation from the current Timeline.

4.1.4 Modifying Already-Created Animations

Edge Animate lets you change all animations after they have been created. To change the properties of a keyframe, simply move the playhead to the position on the Timeline and change the property settings, either in the Property panel, on the lane level within the Timeline, or directly on the Stage.

The duration of an animation sequence can be changed directly in the Timeline. Your cursor displays as a hand pointer, indicating that you can move the keyframe. Simply move one of the keyframes in an animation lane. Only the currently selected keyframe is moved while all others remain in place. If you want to stretch or compress an entire animation span with multiple lanes and keyframes as a whole, select the animation track above the keyframes and use the double-headed arrow to shorten or lengthen it. In this process, all child animations are recalculated.

✎ **Selecting keyframes**

In order to select the right keyframe, make sure Snapping is enabled. Otherwise, you might accidentally select a point on the Timeline before or after your intended keyframe, especially when the Timeline is zoomed out. This creates an additional keyframe, often creating unintended jumps within the animation.

Figure 4.7
The timing of an animation can be changed directly in the Timeline with various sliders and cursors

4.2   Non-Linear Animation—Easing

The techniques we have covered thus far can already produce more complex animations, but you will quickly notice that the animations often feel lifeless or unnatural. This is because the standard linear interpolation used to create the animations makes them look very mechanical. A linear interpolation calculates the intermediate values between two keyframes so that they are evenly spread. Thus, an animation begins at full speed, retains its initial tempo, and then ends abruptly. Such animations appear unnatural because linear motion hardly ever occurs in real life. In most cases, we are dealing with much more complex movements that involve acceleration and deceleration. When an object moves, a change to its state takes place, which, in animation, is known as easing. While linear movement looks mechanical, acceleration from stillness and the subsequent deceleration back to stillness convey naturalness. The following section covers how to simulate these processes. To change the tempo of an animation span, so-called easing equations are used, which are the basis for calculating intermediate values between states.

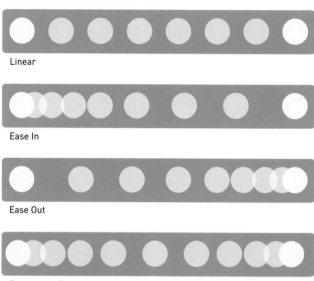

Figure 4.8
While linear movements look mechanical, acceleration and deceleration appear natural

While in the early stages of Flash, creative coders experimented with formulas to get the desired results. People like Robert Penner (http://www.robertpenner.com/easing) have created libraries with many developed easing functions that are available to the web design community. We can take advantage of this resource directly. The figure below shows you all the easing functions contained in Edge Animate. The graph previews greatly simplify the use of easings, making it unnecessary to run trials of many combinations.

Basically, easings comprise three main groups: one group creates acceleration, the second causes deceleration and the third group combines both behaviors so that the animation begins slowly and slows down again at the end. The following figure gives an overview of all available easings in Edge Animate and a graph of their acceleration curve.

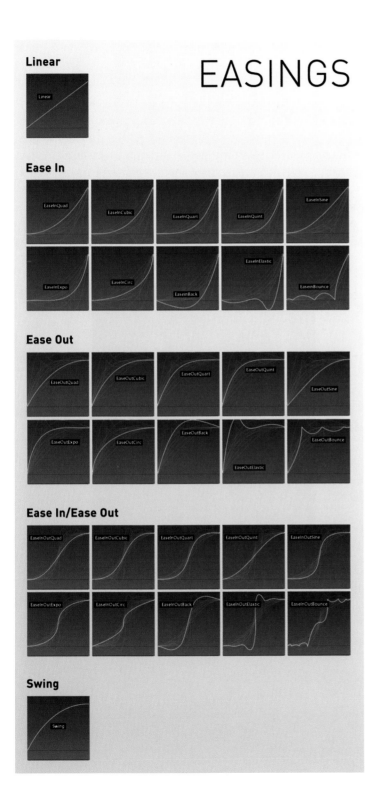

EASINGS

Linear

Ease In

Ease Out

Ease In/Ease Out

Swing

Figure 4.9
Overview of easings for natural, non-linear animation

4.3 Path Animations

One of the biggest innovations in the Edge Animate Creative Cloud (CC) is the integration of motion paths for animations. This method allows you to simulate more complex and authentic movements than those created with the traditional, linear x/y offsets. You can still use this method and the standard settings for animations, but now if you select the Motion Paths option for an element in the Property panel, you can define a motion path to animate the object. You do this in the usual manner, with transitions created by keyframes or the Pin. However, now a line appears with two anchor points that can be reshaped and curved however you choose. This is done by adding an additional anchor that appears when you click on the line. You can also delete these anchors with a mouse click while holding down the Cmd/Ctrl key.

The anchors at the ends of the line are represented by triangles, and the anchors for curving the line are represented by squares. These square anchors are used to adjust the direction and degree of the curve path. The Auto-Orient option sets whether the orientation of the animated element remains fixed or changes along with the curves while following the motion path.

The sample image shows the animation path of the robot's trajectory, which is not linear, but runs in arcs and curves. In addition, an easing effect has been applied to the last path to simulate a deceleration.

Here is a brief overview of how to use motion paths:

▸ Add an anchor: click the path and drag it out
▸ Remove anchor: Cmd/Ctrl + click on the anchor
▸ Change an anchor: click the anchor while holding down the Alt key to toggle between sharp anchors (no Bezier control points) and anchors with control points
▸ Move the entire path: hold down the Cmd/Ctrl key, click on a path section with no anchor points and drag it out to the new position. Grouped paths will also be moved with the clicked path
▸ Adjust the curve: drag a Bezier control point
▸ Disconnect the control points: select the control point while holding down the Alt key, and drag it apart to move it and separate it from its counterpart

Through the use of keyframes (X/Y coordinates), motion paths can be divided into individual segments. If these are removed, the continuous path is restored. Easings can be applied independently to individual segments. In order to spatially separate the segments, click the keyframe anchor while holding down Cmd/Ctrl key and move it. Two separated segments can be connected again by pulling the origin anchor of one path onto the destination anchor of the other. The paths will automatically connect.

The point by which the object follows the motion path is determined by the origin of transformation.

> ✎ **Bezier Curve**
> The Bezier curve is a parametric curve that is an important tool in vector graphics.

4.4   Symbols and Their Timelines

✎ **Symbols and MovieClips**
Symbols in Adobe Edge are comparable to MovieClips in Adobe Flash. They not only combine multiple visual elements, but they also create their own Timeline.

So far you have learned how to create sequential animations on the main Timeline. However, in many cases, this sequential approach is not sufficient; a composition might consist of various independent single animations that are played asynchronously. An example of this is a long character animation in which a second, smaller logo animation is played in a continuous loop, similar to how a TV station logo in the upper right corner of the screen functions. In interactive compositions, you will quickly feel the limits of using a single Timeline. Let us take a closer look at how we can selectively use symbols in Edge Animate to create independent Timelines and their controls.

4.4.1   Symbols

A symbol in Edge Animate is a kind of child composition that consists of individual elements, but that can be moved around the Timeline as one entity and has its own Timeline. Symbols can be nested in any order, making it possible to create a hierarchical structure for compositions.

You can create a symbol on the Stage by selecting one or more existing visual elements and then opening the context menu with a right-click and selecting Convert to Symbol (shortcut: Cmd or Ctrl+Y).

Figure 4.10

Both single elements and groups of elements can be converted into symbols

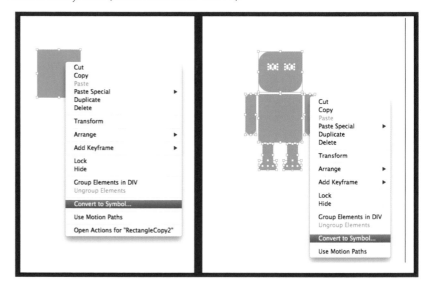

When converting to a symbol, you must designate it with a unique name that is also used to store the new symbol in the Library. Symbol names should be limited to letters, numbers and underscores, as these names may later be used in scripts for actions. In addition, you can also set the playback behavior of the new symbol with the Autoplay Timeline checkbox. If the checkbox is checked (default setting) the symbol's Timeline immediately begins playing as soon as it is placed on the

Stage. If you want to deactivate autoplay, to allow a user interaction, for example, you can simply deselect the option. Of course, you can also change this option in the symbol's Property panel later, as described in section 3.7.5.

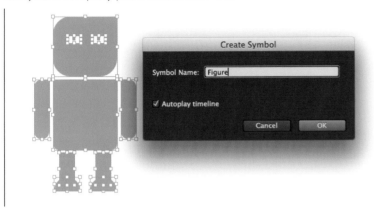

To change the contents of a symbol at a later point, you can open the symbol by double-clicking it on the Stage. Not only does this let you make changes to the elements contained in the symbol, it also gives you access to the symbol's Timeline. Now you can create animations on the symbol's Timeline just like on the composition's main Timeline.

The breadcrumb trail in the upper left corner of the Stage can be used to navigate within the symbols, return to the Stage and the main Timeline, or move between the parent and child levels of the composition.

Figure 4.11
The nesting order of symbols is visible in the upper left

4.4.2 Reusing Symbols

In addition to independent Timelines, symbols have another distinct advantage over simple element groups. Symbols are stored in the Library panel on the right side of the Stage and can be placed on the Stage as often as needed.

Figure 4.12

All symbols within the project are listed in the Library

This procedure is often referred to as inheritance. The symbol is defined in an initial state, which is inherited by all instances positioned on the Stage. You can also change a symbol instance on the Stage for whatever properties you require, such as rescaling. Any changes that you apply directly to the instance on the Stage only affect that particular instance. However, if you change elements or properties within a symbol, any modifications will be applied to all existing instances.

4.4.3 Independent Timelines

If you want to play different animations independently, symbols are the right choice. As already mentioned, each symbol has its own Timeline that is independent from the composition's main Timeline. This makes it easy to create a loop for individual animations, for example. The following example illustrates how the Timelines are independent from one another. The red bar should first grow from left to right, and it needs two seconds to do so. We create this animation directly on the main Timeline (1). However, for the green bar, we first convert it to a symbol so that we can create the growth animation symbol's Timeline (2). When we create the symbol, we check the Autoplay Timeline checkbox so that both bars start to grow at the beginning of the composition. The green bar animation should last five seconds. If we start the composition in the browser, both animations are played completely until the composition stops. However, if we now pause the main Timeline at one second with a trigger (3), the decoupling of the two Timelines becomes visible (you will learn about triggers in section 4.4.5).

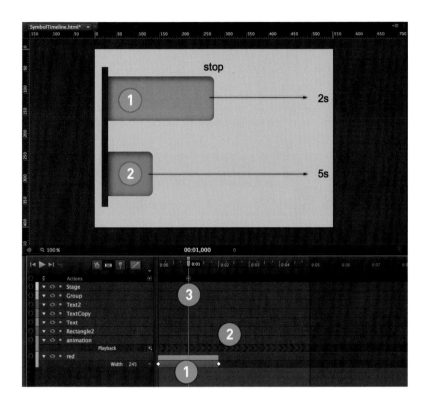

Figure 4.13
Example of independent Timelines

Now when we play the result in the browser, we see that the red bar animation stops halfway. This is the expected result; the trigger is on the same Timeline as the red bar animation so that the stop statement refers exactly to this Timeline. The green bar, however, is not affected because the Timelines are not linked. Thus, an animation within a symbol is played entirely to its end independently from Timeline actions (stop, play or jump), unless explicit statements indicate otherwise within the symbol. In our example, the green bar grows over the defined five seconds while the main Timeline is actually paused. This behavior can be nested in any order by creating additional symbols within a symbol. Section 4.5.3 gives you more information about how to use this technique to create complex animation sequences and loops.

Project
The files for this example can be downloaded from http://edgebuch.simonwidjaja.com
Project Name:
Animation_Symbol_Timeline

4.4.4   Controlling Timelines With Playback Actions
Of course, you do not necessarily always want symbol animations to start immediately and then play to the end. Edge Animate offers two ways to control symbol Timelines. On one hand, you can set playback actions on the Timeline for easy control of subordinate symbol Timelines. Playback actions are nothing more than keyframes that affect the playback behavior of the symbol through six simple statements. This symbol can be stopped, played or played in reverse.

All three commands can either relate to the current position of the internal play-head or refer to an absolute position by adding "from ..." or "at ...".

No additional programming is required for a simple playback. Select the symbol to be changed, and the six commands will be visible in the Property panel on the left side, under the Playback section.

The commands can also be accessed in a separate animation lane in the Timeline. Move the playhead to whatever position you choose on the Timeline, and then assign the playback action by clicking the + icon on the Playback lane.

Figure 4.14

The different playback actions for symbols

The individual playback actions are then visualized by different rectangles directly on the Timeline. They look as follows:

Figure 4.15

Playback actions on various lanes of the Timeline

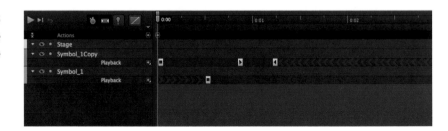

Once you have set several playback actions, you can see the result directly in the preview or by moving the playhead. All playback actions can be viewed here and each action is displayed accordingly. This can be a problem for very complex and computationally intensive animations, since sometimes the display is slow to load. You can also manage the automatic evaluation and rendering of asynchronous animation sequences in the Playback section of the Property panel. Moving the playhead for preview purposes is also called scrubbing. You can toggle this behavior on and off via the Scrub checkbox. This option always only affects the currently selected symbol.

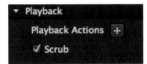

These playback actions can be used to create and control already complex and nested animations. However, animation sequences created in this way are static. In the browser, they are always played back in exactly the same order and with the same animation sequences. Eventually you will have to write code if you want to include interaction or instruct dynamic animations to play back or stop at an unknown time.

4.4.5 Controlling Timelines With Script Statements

If you want to control a Timeline using scripts, you have two options: for one, you can write simple code statements directly on the Timeline and link them to a certain point in time so that they are always executed when the playhead reaches that point. In Edge Animate, these scripts are called triggers. Besides triggers, you can also use events. Unlike triggers, events are not linked to a specific time on the Timeline, but are run by different types of events (click, load progress, focus, etc.). The latter is discussed in section 5.2. Let us first look at how we can control the Timeline through triggers.

Whenever you want to change the behavior of a script, you can add code wherever you see two curly braces ({}). To place a trigger, you must first move the playhead of the specific Timeline to the desired position where the trigger is to be executed. When you click the {} icon that holds a keyframe in the upper right corner of the Timeline level (keyboard shortcut: Ctrl or Cmd+T), Edge Animate's Code panel, the program's component for adding simple scripts, appears. You will learn more about the Code panel in chapter 5.6.

Figure 4.16

Triggers can be directly on the Timeline at the playhead's position

The Code panel contains three important areas:

▸ Panel title: The panel title indicates the exact position of the trigger. This value after the @ sign specifies how many milliseconds there are between the trigger and the starting point of the Timeline in question. Normally this is the starting point of the whole composition. Since symbol Timelines are not linked to the main Timeline, the value after the @ sign refers to the starting point within the symbol.

▸ Code snippets: The code snippets on the right represent a selection of frequently-used statements. These range from Timeline controls to calling an external URL to dealing with symbols, elements, and variables, for advanced coders.

▸ Code area: The white area is the editor for writing code. Here you can manually write code or use one of the many code snippets on the right side. All scripts in Edge Animate are written in JavaScript.

Figure 4.17

A simple action to stop the Timeline within a trigger

All code in Edge Animate, whether written by hand or created using snippets, is enclosed in a function declaration. We see the exact function comments in the gray, shaded line directly above the numbered lines of code. Normally the function signature is as follows:

```
function( sym, e )
```

This means that in your code, you have access to the `sym` variable. This variable is basically a reference to the Stage or the actual Timeline of the parent symbol. This is the reference you need when you want to control the Timeline through code. Edge Animate has its own set of commands to control the Timeline and deal with symbols, known as the Edge Animate API. This command is also provided with the `sym` variable. For example, you can call the Timeline commands `play()` or `stop()` directly on the variable as follows:

```
// stop the Timeline at the given position (ms or label)
sym.stop(0);

// play Timeline from the current
// position
sym.play();
```

If you have no experience in scripting, it is recommended that you take a closer look at the code snippets. Not only does this simplify the work, it also functions like a tutorial. The comments added in the process are very good descriptions of each snippet.

4.5 Lessons

In the lessons section of this chapter, four small projects will teach you how to use and combine different animation techniques with Edge Animate. The sample projects cover:

▸ Banner animation: In this example, we create a simple banner for the header of any page.
▸ Asynchronous animation with playback actions: In this example, we use the playback actions for controlling different Timelines.
▸ Car animation with script-driven Timeline: In this example, we will create a simple car animation that we will temporarily stop, using script, and then play again after a short pause.
▸ Sprite sheet animation: In this example, we will create a sprite sheet that we will use in Edge Animate to create an animation sequence depicting a character running and jumping.

Figure 4.18

Sample project: animation sequence for
a banner

4.5.1   Banner Animation

The first sample project is a simple banner that you can embed in any web page.
The specific example comes from the website edgedocks.com. Three text elements will appear in succession. At the end, the logo will drop in from above.

1. First, create a new composition that fits the required dimensions of the
   website page. In this example, the Stage is 870 x 320 px.
2. As background, simple artwork from Photoshop will suffice, saved as an
   image file and then dragged and dropped onto the Stage with the mouse.
3. For the animated elements, start backwards. First, position all three text
   elements as they should appear at the end of the animation. Since there is
   only one Timeline in this example, you do not need any symbols; you can
   create all the elements directly on the Stage. Depending on design preferences, you can use a white font with a simple drop shadow to make the text
   appear slightly lighter and stand out from the background.
4. Position the animate logo in its end position.
5. Use the Pin to create your animation going backwards. To do this, fix the
   three text elements with the Pin at a half-second (0:005), and then move the
   yellow playhead to the beginning of the Timeline (0:00). To work accurately,
   activate the grid with a resolution of 0.25 seconds. Move all three text elements to the right so that an animation sequence is created in which the
   elements remain in the correct position. In addition, we will fade-in the text
   elements. This should not happen during the entire motion sequence, but
   only after the first half. To do this, leave the Pin activated but move the blue
   pin control to a quarter of a second so that our Pin sequence from 0:00 to
   0:0025 is sufficient. If you set the opacity in the Property panel to 0%, the
   text elements will appear as they move to the left.
6. Since not all text elements should appear simultaneously, let the finished
   text animations play one by one by delaying them each by a quarter of a
   second.

📕 **Project**

The files for this example can be
downloaded from http://edgebuch.
simonwidjaja.com
Project Name:
Animation_Simple Animation

7. Apply similar steps to the logo. Position the playhead at 0:02 seconds, and the Pin behind the playhead at 0:04 seconds. Push the logo up and outside the composition so that it falls into the image from above during the animation. Make sure that the overflow of the composition is set to *hidden* so that the logo is not visible outside of the composition. The animation is now finished, and you can view it in the browser by pressing Ctrl+Enter or Cmd+Enter. Exporting or publishing this banner is explained in chapter 6.

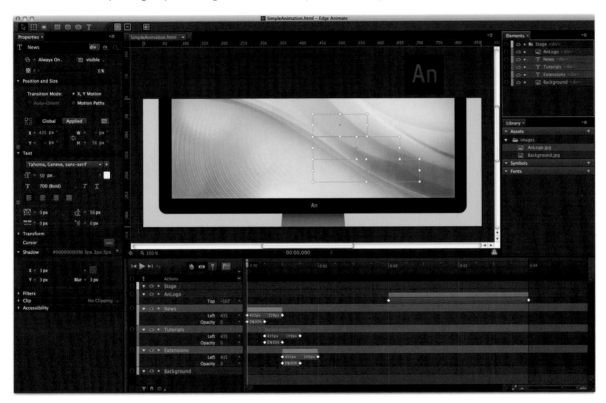

4.5.2 Asynchronous Animation and Playback Actions

For a better understanding of how to work with playback actions, we will create four different animations with animation elements in our second sample project. As the screenshot shows, the end result is a dashboard with four elements. First off, a simple progress bar at the bottom of the composition will be animated. The bar will grow steadily over the total duration of the four-second animation. In the upper area, a number symbol will appear on the left once the composition is started. In the middle, an animated stopwatch will make two complete rotations during the animation. On the right, a vertical bar will fill in as the animation plays out. However, this time the animation will start after one second.

📄 **Project**

The files for this example can be downloaded from http://edgebuch.simonwidjaja.com

Project Name:
Animation_Async_Animation

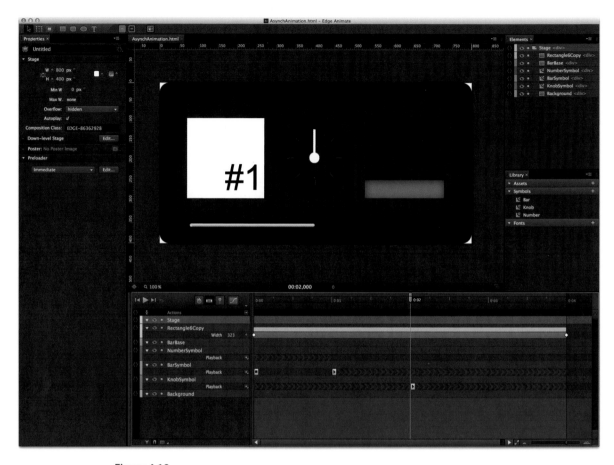

Figure 4.19

Sample project for Asynchronous animations

1. This time, the background is a simple rectangle with rounded corners and an inner shadow to create a slightly more three-dimensional effect.

2. Since the horizontal progress bar at the bottom starts to grow immediately and is active during the entire duration, we can animate it directly in the main Timeline. To do this, simply use the Pin to create an animation over the entire four seconds of the composition.

3. For the rectangle with the number, first create a rectangle on the Stage and use the Text tool to create any arbitrary number. Select both of these elements and convert them into a symbol. Double-click the newly created symbol to animate the opacity of both elements from 0% to 100%. Return to the Stage to see a band of gray arrows pointing to the right; this indicates that hidden animations are stored here in a symbol, which means you cannot directly change individual keyframes from the outside. This makes it possible to create complex animations and depict them in hierarchies.

4. The third element represents a simplified stopwatch that can easily be created with Edge Animate's native tools. To do this, first combine two circles with two different shadows, and then create the dial hand with a number of small rectangles through rotation. The circular dial hand is built with a rectangle and a circle grouped together, and then moved around the face of the bigger circle by moving its origin of transformation. The last step is important so the circle will rotate around this center and not around the center of the group. Now create a symbol from all four levels. Inside the symbol, animate the hand, which should perform a full rotation from 0:00 to 0:02.

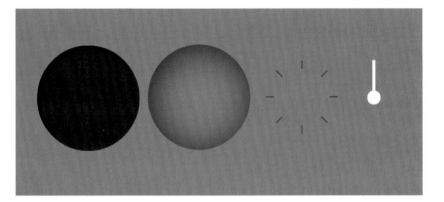

Figure 4.20
A simple stopwatch animation

5. The last element, the vertical bar, is built with two rectangles—one for the background and one for the colored bar. Convert both to a symbol and animate the bar accordingly. The Stage Timeline now looks like this:

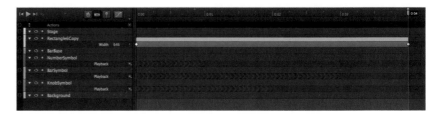

6. As you can see from the band of gray arrows, all symbol animations start at the beginning of the composition and stop well before the end. Now modify the playback behavior of the circular dial hand and the bar animation. For the latter, move the playhead on the Stage Timeline to 0:00 and set the Stop playback action to prevent a direct playback. A stop icon appears on the Timeline, represented by a square within a rectangle. If you move the playhead to the right to 0:01, the symbol will start, delayed via the Play playback action. Wherever an internal animation is stopped, the band of gray arrows disappears from the Timeline.

7. Unlike the other elements, the round dial hand should start immediately and rotate twice around its axis. To do this, move the playhead to the end of the first rotation, or to 0:02 seconds. To achieve a new playback, assign Play From from the playback actions. Unlike the simple Play command, this function gives you the ability to specify an absolute position from which the playback should occur. We use 0:00 so that the playhead of the internal Timeline within the symbol moves at the beginning, and is then played back. You can use this technique to easily play back repetitive animation sequences as often as needed without having to create them multiple times. The final Timeline looks as follows:

Figure 4.21

The final Timeline with animation and Playback commands

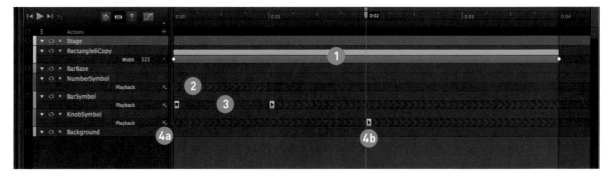

4.5.3 Symbols and Control Through Script

The third sample project uses triggers to control nested symbols. This example illustrates the operation of script-based control through a simple traffic scene in which a car drives into the scene from the left and drives out the right side of the image. A traffic light symbol in the background shows two red lights where the car will stop for one second. The lights turn green, and the car moves again. Up to this point, the main Timeline was sufficient for all the animations, without any additional procedures. Now, even the wheels of the car are supposed to turn in a continuous loop and stop temporarily when the car stops. This is done through the use of nested symbols, which we control from the outside by means of scripts.

Figure 4.22
Sample project for controlling symbols with script

1. First, create a new composition and draw the road and sky with simple rectangles. Simple forms are all that are needed to create the traffic light. Initially, the lights have a red background color. We will use keyframes to switch this to green at about 0:03 seconds.
2. The car is also composed of simple shapes. To make the rotation of the wheels more visible, create them in Photoshop. Designing more complex rims with primitive shapes is too tedious in Edge Animate.
3. Take all parts of the car, including the wheels, and convert them into a symbol by choosing the Convert to Symbol function in the right-click context menu. Name the symbol "car" so that we can modify it later via script. The Autoplay Timeline checkbox is checked. Now we go into the symbol with a double-click and convert the two wheels to a symbol named "tires." Again, double-click the symbol to work within it and create the rotation animation of both wheels on two separate animation lanes.

Project

The files for this example can be downloaded from http://edgebuch. simonwidjaja.com
Project Name: Animation_Car

Figure 4.23

The individual elements of the car symbol

4. When the partial composition is played in the browser, the wheels rotate only once on their axis. To achieve a looping animation of the wheels, go back into the "tires" symbol and move the playhead to the end of the rotation sequence. Place a trigger with the following script to replay the sequence.

Figure 4.24
Trigger and action to replay the symbol Timeline

5. If the animation sequence (in this case, an exactly 360° rotation sequence) starts and stops with the same image, you can use this technique to create animation loops without any optical jumping or stuttering of the images during the transition. View the composition in the browser again, and you'll see that the wheels rotate in a continuous loop.

6. Now we have to stop the rotation sequence when the car stops at the traffic light, and restart them as soon as the light turns green and the car moves again. For this task, return to the Stage Timeline. Here, set the triggers at the right locations, and go into the "car" and "tire" symbols so you can control the Timeline with the `stop()` or `play()` functions. To do this, place a trigger at 0:02 and navigate through the function `getSymbol()` to the correct child symbol.

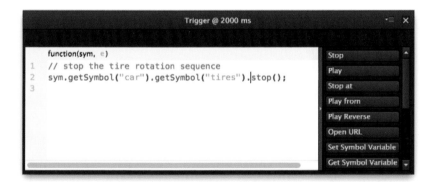

Figure 4.25
Action for stopping the "tire" animation of the child symbol

7. A second later, at 0:03, the car starts driving again and we restart the rotation sequence with a trigger. This time we swap out `stop()` for `play()` so that the sequence continues at the point where it was last stopped.

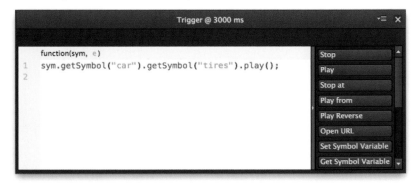

The final Timeline should now look like this: (1) The movement of the car is momentarily stopped, (2) the color of the traffic light glow is shown using a keyframe that changes at (3), and (4) shows the rotation sequence of the tires stop and start, respectively.

Figure 4.26
The final Timeline showing the animation sequence and the trigger points

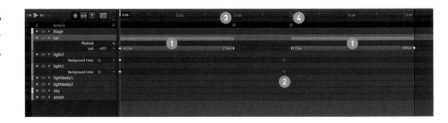

4.5.4   Character Animation With Sprite Sheets

The last example in this chapter shows you how to use Edge Animate for making image sequences with sprite sheets, which is a method for creating animated characters, for instance. Often this technique is used in relation to interactions in gaming. For this example, we will focus on an animation sequence without interaction, but the animation created here could easily be used in an interactive scene as a next step. Sample project 7.5 uses the animation created in this exercise and brings it to life with keyboard commands.

The aim of this example is to create a walking character that enters the screen from the left, moves to a predefined point where it jumps in the air once, and then stays standing at the same spot.

📄 **Project**

The files for this example can be downloaded from http://edgebuch.simonwidjaja.com
Project Name:
Animation_SpriteSheet

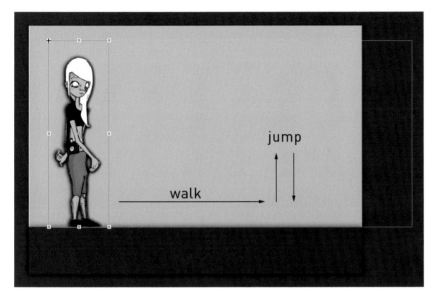

Figure 4.27
The animation sequence for animated characters

1. The starting point for this example is designing the character. You can cre-
    ate any character you want. In this example, we will use the classic method
    and create our figure in Photoshop. You could also use Flash, Illustrator,
    Fireworks, or other graphic programs. Since the first version of Edge Ani-
    mate still cannot read automated sprite sheets with generated position
    information, we will create this manually. To do this, first look at the range
    of motion of the figure to determine the maximum dimensions for all im-
    age variations, which in our case is 100 x 300 px. Use these dimensions to
    create a simple grid in Photoshop with guides or the grid function. In the
    grid, position all the states representing the movement you want to create.
    The following figure shows the movement sequence for walking in the first
    line, and the jump in the second line. Save the final image composition as
    a PNG24 graphic file with alpha channel so you can place the figure on any
    background.

Figure 4.28

Sprite sheet images for the character's walking movements

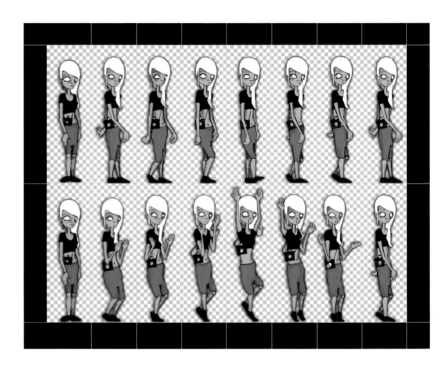

2. Next, create a new Edge Animate project by creating two simple surfaces for the ground and background. In this step, you can also get creative in Photoshop and design an attractive environment. However, for this example, we will just stick to simple rectangles.

3. For the figure, first draw a colored rectangle on the Stage that is the exact dimensions of a grid cell (100 x 300 px) from the sprite sheet. The color does not matter; you only need it to set the dimensions of the character symbol, and you will remove it in a later step.

Figure 4.29

Basic dimensions of the character animation

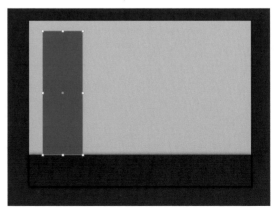

4. Convert the shape into a symbol and call it "character," leaving the Autoplay Timeline box checked. Once the symbol is created, double-click on it to open it, and to place the sprite sheet that was created in Photoshop earlier.

    Position it directly on the top right coordinate origins so that the first character is located exactly in the center of the symbol boundaries. Since we want to use the keyhole effect to always only depict one figure, set the symbol's Overflow property from *visible* to *hidden*. In this way, the figures outside of the symbol borders are not displayed. Finally, remove the colored area.

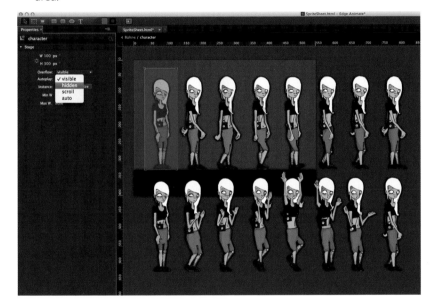

Figure 4.30

The final character sequence

5. Now we start to work on the actual animation sequence. First, manually set a keyframe for the x-coordinate at the beginning of the Timeline, within the symbol. This defines the position of the sprite sheet for the first image and ensures that it is not set in the next step (through an automatic keyframe) with an incorrect value.

6. Now, to make it easier to move the sprite sheet, activate the Timeline grid with 10 fps grid increments. This grid works together with Timeline snapping to exactly position the individual images. Now we can create a new keyframe for each image and move the sprite sheet horizontally along each position to process all the walking sequence frames.

7. Generate a continuous loop for the walking sequence by adding a label (named "walk") to the second keyframe, which is the first image of the walking sequence. At the last image, we set a trigger that uses the command `sym.play ("walk") ;` to create the animated loop. When the composition starts in the browser, we can already see the figure walking in place.

Figure 4.31
The walking sequence as a continuous loop

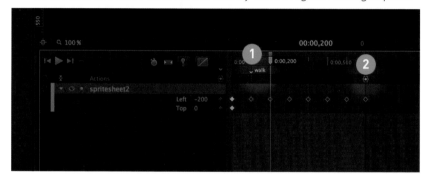

8. Now we build out the movement sequence with the jump. To do this, move the sprite sheet vertically upward to view the second line. Move the sprite sheet across the images, creating a keyframe for each one as we proceed. Finally, add another label, called "jump," so that we can activate the jumping sequence later. Because the animation is set up as a continuous loop, the jump sequence never runs independently. This completes the steps for creating the character's movement sequence.

Figure 4.32
Labels for the walking and jumping sequences

9. On the main Timeline, we can now have the character walk into the image through a simple horizontal animation and come to a stop after about two seconds. The walking sequence is run automatically up to that point. If the character is immediately animated to about 100 px upward and then downward again, the jumping motion is created but the motion sequence itself will still not play. To achieve this, move the playhead to the first frame of the jumping movement, and apply a playback action. Select Play From. This time, do not use a specific time value but rather the "jump" label you created earlier. This instructs the character to perform the jumping sequence.

10. This completes the sprite sheet animation. The final Timeline should look like this:

Figure 4.33
Starting the jumping sequence through playback actions

5

Interactivity and *Scripting*

5 Interactivity and Scripting

✎ Browser Console

The console of a browser can receive simple test messages sent from the currently open web page. These provide abstract information on the inner life of an Edge Animate Composition.

When using interactivity in your Edge Animate composition, three components come into play: actions (scripts), triggers, which we introduced in the last chapter, and events. Events are similar to triggers, but with one fundamental difference: events depend on external circumstances rather than simply taking place at a specific time. They can be initiated by the system user or by internal processes. If you want reactions to external occurrences, events are the right approach.

An interaction has two basic parts: the action that should actually happen, and the point in time at which the action should happen. Edge Animate offers many actions through the Edge Animate API. The Edge Animate API is based on the popular JavaScript jQuery library, making it easy to add extensions.

5.1 Simple Logging

✎ Comparison to Flash

Calling `console.log()` is roughly equivalent to using the `trace()` function from the Flash world; this is often used for Flash movies with complex interaction, for better understanding interconnections.

Before we explore scripting in Edge Animate, let's first have a look at logging. A typical procedure for creating interactivity is logging calls, which is similar to setting traces. To do this, you send simple text messages to the browser's console to ensure that the code is called at the right time. This procedure is especially well established in the Flash world. For simple interactions, you don't necessarily need to use this method. However, logging is helpful with complex and nested user interactions that can happen asynchronously. The following example gives a basic idea of the JavaScript `console.log()` method in a sample Edge Animate composition.

We can assume that the composition itself will send a message to the browser's debugging console as soon as it is loaded (`compositionReady` event). In addition, there are two buttons that also send a message to the console via `console.log()` when the buttons are clicked.

The following code example is meant to give a rough understanding of logging. For instructions on how to actually create such code, see 5.5.11. Suppose we write the following comments in the relevant events:

```
//Log statement in compositionReady event
console.log ( "Composition is ready");

//Log statement click event of the first button
console.log ( "First button was clicked." );

//Log statement click event of the second button
console.log( "Second button was clicked." );
```

If we now start the final composition in a browser such as Google Chrome and open the debugging console (Windows: Ctrl+Shift+J, OS X: Cmd+Alt+J), the output for the logging statements are as follows:

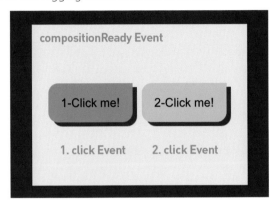

Figure 5.1
Overview of the events (blue text) displayed in the console

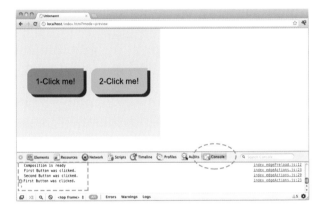

Figure 5.2
Simple logging with `console.log()` and the ouput in the Google Chrome console

However, `console.log()` should only be used in the development of a page. Logging reveals many details about your composition, but with frequent use, it can affect the playback speed of the animations. Also note that this feature is not available in certain browsers, such as in older versions of Internet Explorer, which can result in subsequent scripts not being executed as expected. Another disadvantage of `console.log()` is the fact that while you can use different log levels (`info, debug, warning` and `error`), these are extremely difficult to filter. Also, subsequent deactivation of log-levels is not possible. To avoid these problems, I recommend you to take a look at the logging functions of the free Edge Commons extension.

Project

The files for this example can be downloaded from http://edgebuch. simonwidjaja.com
Project Name:
Interaction_Simple_Logging

5.2   Events

Events, which are executed or fired when a composition is played, are an essential part of an interactive user interface. You can specifically listen to these events in order to respond accordingly through the use of code. Events can be caused by the user, the composition, or the Timeline, but also by triggers within the animation and the host system, such as the reloading of data. There are six types of events:

1.   User events
2.   Composition events
3.   Timeline events
4.   Triggers (special types of Timeline events)
5.   Symbol events
6.   System events (mostly jQuery events)

Specific examples of different event types:

▶ User events • The user moves the mouse over a button, or clicks on a thumbnail.

▶ Composition events • The composition was created successfully and can execute code, or the displaying device is rotated so that the display type (orientation) adjusts accordingly.

▶ Trigger • You can manually define a trigger anywhere on the Timeline that will execute whatever code you choose when the playhead reaches the trigger's point.

▶ Timeline events • The Timeline starts or stops the playback. You can listen to the movement of the playhead through an event.

▶ Symbol events • A symbol from the Library is created or deleted.

▶ System events • In most cases, this type of event is not directly triggered by Edge Animate, but by the underlying system. Since Edge Animate internally uses the jQuery framework and `yepnope.js`, these can also fire different events. A typical case is the reloading of a JavaScript or CSS file. In this case, you can wait for the event, which indicates that the external file has successfully loaded, and then proceed with further processing.

5.2.1 Responding to Events

To understand better how to deal with events, we are reproducing the logging example in which the composition event `compositionReady` and the user event `click` are used. In response to the events, a text output will be displayed in the console. To listen to an event in Edge Animate, directly select the element on the Stage and then choose Open Actions for XYZ in the right-click context menu.

Figure 5.3

Dialog for opening the Code panel to create actions for a particular element

In addition, the Edge Animate user interface contains three different double curly braces ({}) that can be used to access the Code panel for events and actions. If the braces are empty, no code has been created. If the braces are filled in, actions for at least one event have been created.

When you open the actions with the right-click menu or the curly braces icon, the Code panel for actions opens. Initially, it only contains the message, "add an event to start coding." Note that the Code panel for actions only applies to the selected element. Since the Stage is ultimately an element or symbol, the Code panel for actions is opened for the Stage if no specific element is selected. Before we can start writing actions, we must first define which event will trigger the action. Use the + icon in the upper left corner to see the available events for the selected element. The following figure shows an example of the possible events for the Stage.

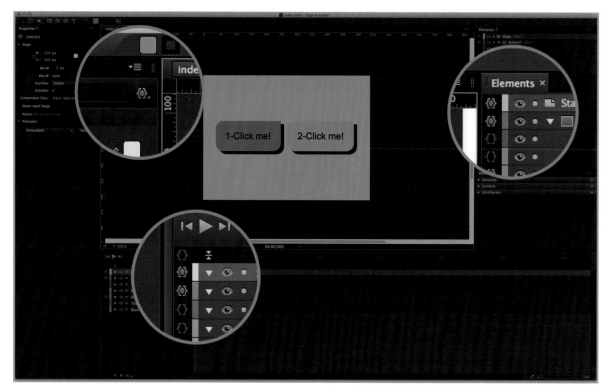

Figure 5.4
The curly braces open the Code panel
for the selected element

Figure 5.5
Use the + icon to add more events

In contrast, only events available for elements are displayed for our button.

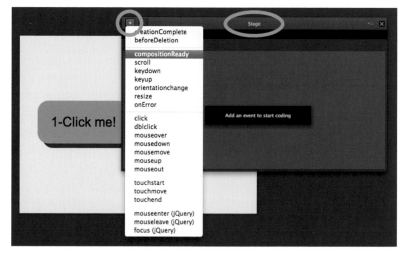

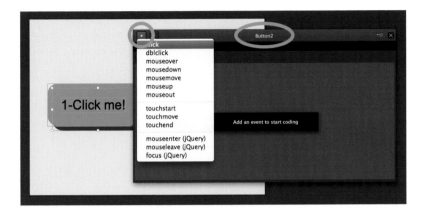

Use the + button to add various events successively. For our logging example, select the click event for the first button, and the corresponding Code panel appears. We can now write any JavaScript code that will always run whenever the event occurs. The code lines preceded by two slashes (//) are comments and are automatically generated by Edge Animate. Now we can write the following logging statement in the code editor:

```
console.log( "First Button was clicked." );
```

Figure 5.6

An initial logging statement for the click event of a button

We now start the composition in the browser and activate the debugging console (Windows: Ctrl+Shift+J, OS X: Cmd+Alt+J). The console will give information about the occurrence of every event every time an element is clicked. To complete the previous example, we add two additional actions: one for the `click` event of the second button and one for the `compositionReady` event of the Stage itself. Through this procedure, you can make sure that the interrelations between all your elements work together behind the scenes before you add more complex actions.

5.2.2   User Events

Now let's take a look at which user events are available to receive instructions from the user, via the mouse, keyboard, or even a touch screen.

For all elements, the following mouse events are available:

▸ click • This event is fired as soon as the user clicks on the element.

▸ dblclick • Similar to `click`, only in this case, a double-click is the event trigger.

▸ mouseover • This event fires as soon as the mouse pointer touches or hovers over the particular element. For this event, you must be aware that it is also activated when a child element is entered within the outer element. This can cause unexpected results and is not suitable for elements such as buttons with multiple levels (e.g., base level and text level). For such cases, use the `mouseenter` event.

▸ mouseout • Opposite to `mouseover`, this event fires as soon as the mouse leaves the element. The same problems that occur with `mouseover` can also happen with this event. To avoid this, you can use the `mouseleave` event.

▸ mouseenter • This event fires once when the mouse enters an element, and then again when the mouse has actually left the surface area of the element. Child elements do not affect this event.

▸ mouseleave • Similar to `mouseenter`, this event is executed once when the mouse leaves an element. Child elements are also not involved in this event.

▸ mousedown and mouseup • When a simple click is not enough because you want to handle the click process in individual phases, these two events are the right solution. `mousedown` is fired as soon as the mouse button is pressed while `mouseup` executes when the mouse button is released. The exact order of a click process is as follows: `mousedown >>> mouseup >>> click`.

▸ mousemove • This event runs continuously while the mouse moves over an element. In the console, the following logging statement `console.log(e.offsetX+" / "+e.offsetY)` gives a live report of the mouse's current coordinates relative to the upper left corner of the involved element.

Additionally, the following events are available for touch screens:

▶ touchstart · This event fires when the finger touches an element on the touch screen.

▶ touchmove · The `touchmove` event runs continuously when the finger moves on the touchscreen after `touchstart`. This event can be used to create functions such as drag & drop.

▶ touchend · This event fires when the finger no longer has contact with the touchscreen.

Be aware that with the `touchstart` event, the `click` event is also fired, but touch events will not additionally run in the desktop environment. If you want to activate an element in a composition with a click on both the desktop and on a touch device like the iPad, it can easily happen that the function is performed twice in a row on the touch device. You can prevent this on touch devices by binding any further execution of the touchstart event so that no additional `click` event is called. You can do this by running the `preventDefault()` function on the event object in the `touchstart` event:

```
e.preventDefault();
```

This workaround is not appropriate in all cases because it can bind other gestures, such as zooming and scrolling. If you want more control over touch behavior and other gestures, take a look at the Hammer.js JavaScript library, which is also available as a jQuery plug-in, as well as in other formats. This extension resolves many problems associated with dealing with gestures.

Figure 5.7
The external Hammer.js JavaScript library provides a solid basis for gesture recognition

If you want to use jQuery extensions that are not supported by Edge Animate, you have to bypass the program's native Actions code panel and work on a deeper level to get direct access to additional jQuery functionality. In chapter 7, you will learn more about the extension possibilities of Edge Animate.

While the events outlined above are available both for the Stage and for all elements and symbols, there are another five events that can only occur at the page level:

▶ swipe · Starting with Edge Animate Creative Cloud, it is now possible to declare left and right swipes as an event for an element. The event is run when the user finger-swipes the element or the Stage on a touch screen.

▶ scroll (page level) · The `scroll` event fires when the user scrolls within the composition.

▶ keydown and keyup (page level) · This event fires when a key is pressed or released. It is used to create keyboard shortcuts or game controls. An example of this event is presented in section 7.5.

▶ resize (page level) · The `resize` event is fired as soon as the size of the browser window changes. This event is often used for responsive design.

▶ orientationChange (page level) · This event is run on mobile devices. When the device is rotated, the screen orientation changes. Use this event if the composition needs to react to the event, such as with different layouts for landscape and portrait.

5.2.3   Composition Events

In addition to user-events, there are also two events for the composition itself:

▶ compositionReady · After the composition is initialized, the `compositionReady` event fires. This event can be used for further preparation of the composition through code. For example, you can use this event when you are setting initial values for variables, or when additional extensions are loaded.

▶ onError · This event is a global error handler and is always called when the code for some other event produces a JavaScript error. This event is global and effects all compositions. This means that all event handlers are called for the `onError` event on a page, regardless of how many compositions are on the page. The argument `compId` provides information about which composition produced the error. Moreover, `e.originalEvent` includes a reference to the original event that caused the error, which is necessary for targeted error handling

5.2.4 Timeline Events

Besides triggers, the Timeline has other asynchronous events that can be fired in connection with the playhead:

▶ play • The play event fires when a stopped playhead is played again.

▶ stop • The stop event fires when the playhead is paused.

▶ update • This event runs continuously when the playhead moves on its Timeline. You should use actions very sparingly here because the performance will suffer when elaborate operations are run several times a second.

▶ complete • The complete event fires once when the playhead reaches the end of its Timeline.

All events are available within any Timeline, although they are somewhat hidden. To add actions to these events, you need to click on the curly braces at the top left of that particular Timeline.

Figure 5.8
Timeline events can be added in the upper left corner of the Timeline via the curly braces icon

5.2.5 Symbol Events

Timeline events are also available to symbols, since a symbol has its own Timeline. In addition, two other events from the Library give information about how a symbol was created:

▶ creationComplete • The creationComplete event fires when a symbol from the Library is made into an instance. Here, initialization statements can be defined that should fire when a symbol is created.

▶ beforeDeletion • In comparison, the beforeDeletion event can be used to clean up the Stage when a symbol is removed.

Both events can only be handled on the symbol level. For that reason, you must first open the symbol (e.g., by double-clicking on the Stage or in the Library) and then click the curly braces icon in the symbol's Property panel.

Figure 5.9

Currently there are only two symbol
events: creationComplete and
beforeDeletion

✎ **yepnope.js**

The yepnope.js library provides
functions for the conditional loading
of JavaScript and CSS files, classifying
it in the Conditional Loader genre.
Yepnope.js is already integrated into
every Edge Animate composition
and does not have to be manually
reloaded.

5.2.6   System Events

▶ jQuery events • When working with symbols and actions, you also have access to jQuery references, which in turn can fire jQuery specific events.

▶ yepnope callback • In addition to jQuery, you also have use of the yepnope loading library, which not only loads individual Edge Animate files at run time, but also runs external JavaScript libraries and style sheets. Since loading is also asynchronous (in other words, not immediately completed after it is called), additional system events can be used here that can be handled as callbacks. The following example illustrates this: first, the destination address is defined with the load key. A function is defined as a callback, which is then fired when loading is complete. Since it involves an external source and the server requires a certain reaction time, loading will definitely happen at a later time.

```
yepnope({
    load: "http://cdn.edgecommons.org/an/1.0.0/js/min/
EdgeCommons.js",
    complete: function() {
        // Your code
        // (e.g. start playing the composition)
    }
});
```

5.3 Context of Events

For experienced JavaScript programmers, the context in which actual code is executed is an interesting issue. As you can see in the screenshot, the gray shaded lines above the code contain a function definition. The entire function to listen to the event (event handler) with our added code looks like this:

```
function(sym, e) {
   // Insert code for mouseclick here
   console.log( "First Button was clicked." );
   console.debug("sym: ", e);
   console.debug("e: ", e);
}
```

In the function signature, we see that two arguments are passed to the function. As we already learned, `sym` returns a reference to the actual symbol, which we can use to change the symbol itself or add more elements. However, the `e argument` refers to the original event object that fired the event. This may be a `mouseevent-type` jQuery event. The can be useful, for example, in evaluating the mouse coordinates for a click. To offer a better understanding of the two arguments on a test basis, we can also output both variables to the console in additional logging statements. For a `click` event, the console output looks like this:

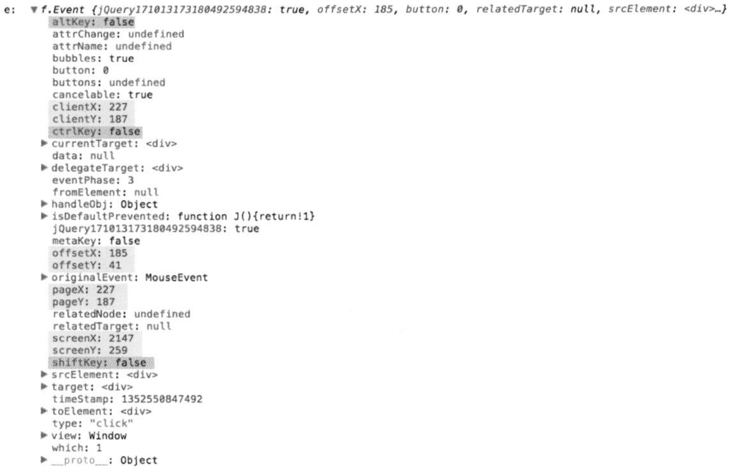

```
e:  ▼f.Event {jQuery171013173180492594838: true, offsetX: 185, button: 0, relatedTarget: null, srcElement: <div>…}
      altKey: false
      attrChange: undefined
      attrName: undefined
      bubbles: true
      button: 0
      buttons: undefined
      cancelable: true
      clientX: 227
      clientY: 187
      ctrlKey: false
    ▶ currentTarget: <div>
      data: null
    ▶ delegateTarget: <div>
      eventPhase: 3
      fromElement: null
    ▶ handleObj: Object
    ▶ isDefaultPrevented: function J(){return!1}
      jQuery171013173180492594838: true
      metaKey: false
      offsetX: 185
      offsetY: 41
    ▶ originalEvent: MouseEvent
      pageX: 227
      pageY: 187
      relatedNode: undefined
      relatedTarget: null
      screenX: 2147
      screenY: 259
      shiftKey: false
    ▶ srcElement: <div>
    ▶ target: <div>
      timeStamp: 1352550847492
    ▶ toElement: <div>
      type: "click"
    ▶ view: Window
      which: 1
    ▶ __proto__: Object
```

Figure 5.10

The click event in the Google Chrome console. The properties in blue provide additional information about coordinates while the red lines refer to possible additional pressed function keys.

The actual assignment of the above-mentioned functions to the corresponding event of an element looks as follows:

Figure 5.11

The parent context of an action

```
8
9   Symbol.bindElementAction(compId, symbolName, "${_Button1}", "click", function(sym, e) {
10      // embed code for mouse click here
11      console.log( "First Button was clicked." );
12      console.debug("sym: ", e);
13      console.debug("e: ", e);
14
15  });
16  //Edge binding end
17
```

5.4   Symbols and Elements

Now you know all the events that may occur in the course of an interactive composition. Before we look at how to create actions that change visual elements, control Timelines, and achieve other interactivity, such as calling a URL, we will first look at the structure of visual elements within Edge Animate. It is essential to differentiate between symbols and elements in order to understand the Edge Animate API.

If you place a rectangle, a circle, or a text element on the Stage, you are initially creating a simple element. The same applies to the placement of an image. Depending on the tag selected, the composition is attached to the corresponding HTML object in the DOM during runtime. Elements are therefore a 1:1 mapping of the HTML objects.

Figure 5.12

For texts and images, different HTML tags can be selected

An element in Edge Animate is a visual object that is represented in classic HTML. The element has the typical HTML/CSS properties, but not a Timeline.

Symbols, however, are strictly non-visual components of Edge Animate. You can imagine a symbol as a kind of element group, which can be stored with its own Timeline in the Library, and made into instances on the Stage as many times as you choose. Since a symbol must always be generated from one or more existing elements, each symbol has at least one element that makes it visible in the first place.

When converting an element into a symbol, the element is not actually changed, but packaged in a symbol container. This means it is removed from its original Timeline and re-assigned to the new Timeline inside the symbol. The symbol container itself is a native Edge Animate construct that provides various functions (Edge Animate API) to access child elements and navigate in the composition hierarchy, such as accessing the parent symbol.

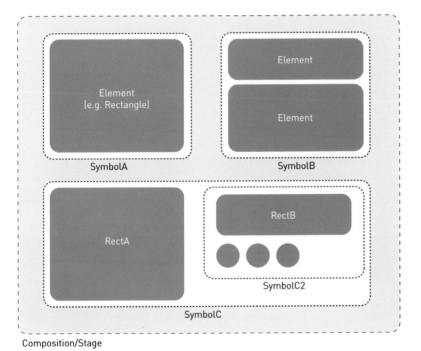

Figure 5.13
Standard nesting of elements and symbols

5.5   Actions

Equipped with an understanding of elements and symbols, we can now turn our attention to actions. The Edge Animate API is the basis for most of the actions you will program in Edge Animate. This API provides all functions for the Timelines and symbols. The official, though rudimentary, documentation can be found at:

http://www.adobe.com/devnet-docs/edgeanimate/api/current/index.html

For that reason, we will now take a look at the individual action commands in detail before we program specific actions.

5.5.1   Code Snippets

The right side of Edge Animate's actions Code panel contains a selection of frequently used commands known as code snippets. Select a snippet and it is inserted on the left side of the panel at the cursor's position. Most snippets use placeholders that you manually have to adapt to the specific situation.

Figure 5.14
Action code snippets in the Edge Animate Code panel

5.5.2 Controlling the Timeline

You already learned simple methods for controlling the Timeline in chapter 4. Here is a complete overview of the various actions and their function signatures. The comments above a given action are automatically added by the Edge Animate snippets function to make the action clear.

You can use the actions `stop()` and `play()` to stop and play a Timeline. Both actions can be called separately. If no argument is passed, the actions relate to the current position of the playhead. In addition, you can pass an argument for both actions. This argument can be either an integer or a string. For an integer, the value is interpreted in milliseconds and the playhead is moved to the absolute position on the Timeline before stopping or playing. For a string, the playhead jumps to the label. Make sure to use correct spelling for labels. If there is no label, the action has no effect, and no error is reported.

```
// Stop and play Timeline
sym.stop();
sym.play();
```

```
// Timeline at the specified position
// stop (ms or name)
sym.stop(1000);
sym.stop("final");
```

```
// Timeline from the specified position
// Play (ms or label)
sym.play (1000);
sym.play("intro");
```

You can also play a Timeline backward from the current position by using the following action:

```
// Play in reverse
sym.playReverse();
```

The object reference `sym` is always a reference to any symbol. Instead of the object reference sym, you can also use a reference to every symbol to control its Timeline. Suppose you placed a symbol animation on the Stage called `MySymbol`. You can play the symbol Timeline from the Stage (e.g. within a `click` event) as follows:

```
// Play Timeline of a child symbol
sym.getSymbol("mySymbol").play();
```

And of course, all Timeline functions are available: (`stop()`, `stop(value)`, `play()`, `play(value)`, and `playReverse()`). More information on navigating through the symbols within a composition is presented in sections 5.5.4 and 5.5.5.

To control the Timeline, you often need additional information, such as the total duration of the animation and playhead state. The Edge Animate API provides a few useful functions. For example, to determine the current position of the playhead in a symbol instance, use the following function. The function returns the value in milliseconds.

```
// Determine current position
var myPos = sym.getPosition();
```

This value is often used in relation to the total time, which you can get in the following way:

```
// Determine total duration of a Timeline
var myDur = sym.getDuration();
```

In some cases, actions vary depending on the state of a Timeline. If you want to determine whether a Timeline is playing, you can use the `isPlaying()` function.

```
// Check state of a Timeline
var myState = sym.isPlaying();
```

This function returns a Boolean value, either true or false. This value can then be further processed, for example, within an if statement:

```
if ( sym.getSymbol("intro").isPlaying() ) {
    console.log("Intro is still playing...");
}
else {
    console.log("Intro is done...");
  }
```

Together with `sym.playReverse()`, you can additionally examine whether the Timeline is currently playing backwards. The function `isPlaying()` returns `true` again.

```
// Check if a Timeline is played backwards
var myStage = sym.isPlayDirectionReverse();
```

If you need the absolute position of a previously defined label in milliseconds, this can be determined using the following function:

```
// Determine the absolute position of a label
var myPos = sym.getLabelPosition (label);
```

The function `sym.getLabelPosition()` returns the value `undefined` if the value cannot be determined. This can be used to check if a label exists, for instance.

```
if (sym.getLabelPosition (label) ) {
   alert ("Label does not exist: "+ Label);
 }
```

5.5.3   Calling a URL

For the insertion of external links, we can use the browser JavaScript function. For example, we can use the following code to open the edgedocks.com website in the same window:

```
// Navigate to a new URL in the current window
// ("_self" replace with new window through
// corresponding target attribute)
window.open("http://www.edgedocks.com", "_self");
```

Based on the target attribute "`_self`", this will replace our composition with the target address. If you want to prevent this and open the URL in a new window or tab, you can use the target attribute "`_blank`".

5.5.4   Accessing Symbols

An Edge Animate composition is basically hierarchical. In other words, all symbols are organized in the Stage's tree structure and can be nested in any order. When you are working in actions, you will often need to navigate through this tree structure. It is important here to distinguish between elements and symbols. While symbols are solely defined and accessed through the Edge Animate API, elements are simply jQuery object references. Let us first look at how we access symbols. The following section of code comes from a code snippet provided by Edge Animate.

```
// Search for JavaScript object for Edge Animate
// symbol in an element that is an instance of a symbol.
```

```
// The symbol object icon can be used to call
// symbol functions such as play stop
 var mySymbolObject = sym.getSymbol("Symbol1");
```

The call `sym.getSymbol(SYMBOLNAME)` is the reference to the symbol, which in this case is a child element of the current Timeline or current symbol. Remember that the current symbol may be the Stage itself. The return value is also a symbol reference. If the symbol contains more symbols, you can use the `getSymbol()` function again to go into a deeper symbol level. Suppose we have the following symbol composition:

Figure 5.15

The inner life of a symbol

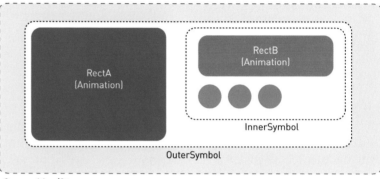

We are on the Stage and want to reference the `OuterSymbol` to play its Timeline. This is done as follows:

```
var myOuterSym = sym.getSymbol("OuterSymbol");
myOuterSym.play();
```

Since the function `getSymbol()` returns a symbol reference, we can also use the following shorthand, as long as we do not reuse the reference in another action:

```
sym.getSymbol("OuterSymbol").play();
```

However, if we want to start the nested red animation, which is additionally embedded in the `InnerSymbol` symbol, the code is as follows:

```
var myOuterSym = sym.getSymbol("OuterSymbol");
var myInnerSym = myOuterSym.getSymbol("InnerSymbol");
myInnerSym.play();
```

Of course, we can also use the shorthand:

```
sym.getSymbol("OuterSymbol")
   .getSymbol("InnerSymbol")
   .play();
```

If you are already inside a symbol and want to access the parent symbol, you can do so with the following expression:

```
// Reference to the parent symbol
   sym.getParentSymbol();
```

If, for example, you are within an intro symbol and want to play the parent Timeline at the end of the Timeline through a trigger action, the action looks like this:

```
sym.getParentSymbol().play();
```

However, with the `getParentSymbol()` function you can only go one level higher, relative to the current Timeline. Of course, you can nest this function however you want, since it returns a symbol, but you should avoid the following code cascade for functions such as accessing the Stage:

```
var stage = sym.getParentSymbol().getParentSymbol();
```

Not only does this quickly create "spaghetti code," it makes it very difficult to restructure your composition. If an affected symbol must be moved into a new symbol, all paths are no longer valid, which in turn creates the need for extra testing and adjustments. For such cases, the Edge Animate API offers an absolute means to access the Stage. You must first determine the actual composition that contains the symbol. This is necessary because multiple stages and their child elements can exist on a page. The function `sym.getComposition()` allows us to access the composition from within each symbol. The returned composition object makes the `getStage()` function available, with which we obtain the reference to the current Stage. Thus, for example, with the following action, we can play all levels of our composition from the film symbol, which is located directly on the Stage.

```
sym.getComposition()
   .getStage()
   .getSymbol("Film")
   .play();
```

For dynamic compositions in which the number of symbol instances is not static, it may be necessary to determine all the Stage's child symbols during runtime. This can occur if the user is able to create symbols through actions during runtime. In such a scenario, it may be necessary to check or prevent issues such as collisions among elements (see section 7.5). For these cases, each symbol has the `getChildSymbols()` function with which you can get references to any child symbol as an array.

```
// Find all child symbols
var symbolArray = sym.getChildSymbols();
```

If you want to stop all child symbols, use the following script:

```
// Stop all direct child symbols
var symbolArray = sym.getChildSymbols();
for(var i=0; i<symbolArray.length; i++) {
   symbolArray[i].stop();
 }
```

5.5.5   Accessing Elements

As already described, the visual components of a symbol consist of elements that are represented by a jQuery object. This means you can also access individual elements with jQuery syntax. Since each element is ultimately located within a symbol, namely in the Stage itself or in a symbol within the Library, elements can also be accessed through the parent symbol. The typical jQuery selector syntax with the $ sign is used to access an element:

```
sym.$("ElementName");
```

However, the only difference to a classic jQuery selector is that neither the class (.) nor the Id prefix (#) is required. This is because the function provided through the $() symbol is not identical to the actual jQuery function, but rather, makes this available in an expanded form. The actual IDs stored in the DOM are much longer. They begin with the prefix "Stage_" and add it as another identifier to each level in the symbol tree hierarchy. Thus, the actual ID of an element ("MyElement"), which is contained within a symbol ("MySymbol") on the Stage is as follows:

```
Stage_MySymbol_MyElement
```

In order not to lose track, we do not need to use Edge Animate's selector function on the actual path. You only need to specify the element name.

Suppose we use the following symbol composition, in which we want to access three different elements with the selector function in order to hide them:

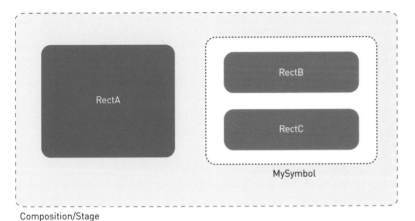

Figure 5.16
A representative symbol composition with child elements

To save a reference of a child element as a variable, we need to formulate the statement as follows:

```
// sym.$("name") folds an Edge Animate element name
// into a DOM element that can be used
// with jQuery.
var element = sym.$("ELEMENTNAME");
```

Here also, the selector function is provided by each symbol, so you can nest the call however you choose. Suppose you want to hide the blue element ("RectA"). The statement then looks as follows:

```
var element = sym.$("RectA");
element.hide();
```

Since the selector function returns a full jQuery object, you can use shorthand here if you do not need the reference for other actions:

```
sym.$("RectA").hide();
```

If, however, you want to hide the red elements within the symbol ("MySymbol"), the statement should read as follows:

```
var symbol = sym.getSymbol("MySymbol");
var element = symbol.$("RectB");
element.hide();
```

or in shorthand:

```
sym.getSymbol("MySymbol").$(:RectB").hide();
```

As mentioned earlier, a symbol instance has no visible elements. However, the symbol container is also a DOM element, namely an invisible DIV container. This is needed for functions such as grouping and moving all symbol content. In addition, this container defines overflow and corresponding scroll behavior. In a few cases, it may be necessary to access this container as an element. To do this, you can use the `getSymbolElement()` symbol function:

```
// Call JQuery handle for the element of a
// JavaScript object for Edge Animate symbol.
var symbolElement = sym.getSymbolElement();
```

5.5.6   Modifying Elements

Let's look at the various ways to modify existing elements. While for symbols we mostly looked at controlling the Timelines, elements are more about changing visual appearance. Since an element reference is a jQuery object that is also depicted in the DOM (as for every classic HTML website), we have use of nearly all options available through jQuery and CSS. Let's first look at Edge Animate's action code snippets. The following actions apply to basic shapes, text elements, and images.

Any element can be hidden using the function `hide()` and displayed again using the function `show()`.

```
// Hide element.
sym.$("myRectangle").hide();
sym.$("myText").hide();
sym.$("myImage").hide();

// Show element.
sym.$("myRectangle").show();
```

Of course, you can also use other jQuery effects that are not available from Edge Animate as action code snippets, such as letting individual elements appear and disappear abruptly, or fly into the image from above. Such effects can be achieved with the functions `slideUp()`, `slideDown()` and `slideToggle()`:

```
// Move element in and out from the top.
sym.$("Text1").slideUp();
sym.$("Text1").slideDown();
sym.$("Text1").slideToggle();
```

If an element is represented by a container, which is the case for almost all elements in Edge Animate (the only exception is the use of the `img` tag for images), you can also easily change the HTML content of the container. Thus, you can do things like set new text for text elements with the function `html()`:

```
// Change the content of an element.
sym.$("MyText").html("new text");
```

Or, if you want to add text to already existing text, use the `append()` function:

```
sym.$("MyText").append("appended text");
```

This function is not just limited to setting simple texts. The following example demonstrates how to use the `html()`-function to load a whole HTML form in a rectangle created in Edge Animate:

```
sym.$("FormBox").html(
    'Name: <input type="text« /><br/>'
    +'Year of birth'
    +'<select>'
    +' <option value="1950">1950-1959</option>'
    +' <option value="1960">1960-1969</option>'
    +' <option value="1970">1970-1979</option>'
    +' <option value="1980">1980-1989</option>'
    +' <option value="1990">1990-1999</option>'
    +' <option value="2000">2000-2010</option>'
    +'</select>'
);
```

> **📄 Project**
>
> The files for this example can be downloaded from http://edgebuch.simonwidjaja.com
>
> **Project Name:**
> Interaction_HtmlAppend

The three examples in action look as follows:

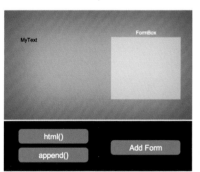 

Figure 5.17
Adding the HTML code in action

In addition to HTML content, the CSS properties can also be changed with code. This may be necessary if you want to use CSS properties that are not supported by Edge Animate. In the following example, a rectangle is to be filled in with a background image that seamlessly repeats in tiles. Edge Animate does not offer a solution for the specific function, so we need to use the `css()` function.

Figure 5.18

A tiled background using CSS

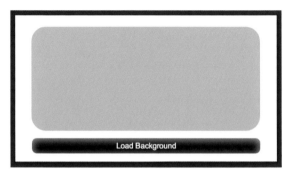

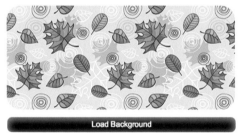

To do this, we first copy our background image (background.png) in the images subfolder of our composition. Draw a new background area as a rectangle on the Stage; name the element "box," and you can assign the background image with the following action. For this we use `sym.$("box")` to get a jQuery reference to the DIV container you created earlier. We can then call the function `css()` for this reference, which takes two arguments. The first argument is the CSS property you want to change, and the second is the value you want to set.

 Project

The files for this example can be downloaded from http://edgebuch. simonwidjaja.com

Project Name:
Interaction_ModifyCSS

```
sym.$("box")
  .css( "background-image",
     "url(images/background.png)"
);
```

In addition to this code variation, Edge Animate offers you yet another way to assign a CSS class to an element. Sticking with the above example, a CSS file could define the following CSS class:

```
.repeatedBackground {
    background-image: url(images/background.png);
}
```

If this CSS file is loaded into the HTML file of an Edge Animate composition, you can assign one or more CSS classes with the small "c" button in the Property panel. Keep in mind that all elements are represented by a DIV container in the DOM, unless you explicitly change them. The CSS properties that you assign in this way will be applied to this DIV container.

Figure 5.19
Add CSS classes to any element

5.5.7 Dynamically Creating and Deleting Symbols

Edge Animate is not just able to create static compositions. You also have the ability to create other dynamic symbol instances at runtime. This can be triggered by user actions or from external data sources. For example, interfaces from server-side applications can be tapped, or data from third parties can be loaded into your composition and then visualized through symbols. Let's have a look at the relevant API.

With the `createChildsymbol()` function, you can create an instance of a previously created symbol that was stored in the Library, and place it on the Stage or inside another existing symbol. Since this function is available for each symbol, we can apply them directly to the `sym` variable. The symbol name is expected as the argument within the Library, followed by the element name of the container where the new symbol instance is to be added.

```
// Instance element of a symbol as child
// Element of the specified parent element
// Create
var mySym = sym.createChildSymbol("Name", "ParentEl");
```

Not only can you create a new symbol instance with script, you can also remove existing symbols in the same manner. The `deleteSymbol()` function is used for this task. It completely deletes the symbol and removes all symbol elements from the DOM. This is currently the only way to clean the Stage's DOM during the course of an animation. Simply disabling or hiding an element or symbol means that the corresponding data in both the DOM and the memory remain intact.

```
// Delete element that is an instance of a symbol.
// (getSymbol searches the object symbol for a
// Symbolinstanceelement)
sym.getSymbol("Symbol1").deleteSymbol();
```

5.5.8   Working with Symbol Variables

For interactive and dynamic compositions, it is often necessary to store values intermittently. On one hand, you have the option to declare a variable within an action as follows:

```
var userName = sym.$("userNameInput").html();
```

If you need the variable only within the action, this local variable is sufficient. Due to the local scope, you cannot access variables from outside, such as from the Stage. As soon as access to the variable from another action or another symbol is required, we need to save the value differently. The need for external access might involve the score in a game, which is stored on the Stage and called from various child symbols.

In such a scenario, you can simply store the values in the global scope, which can be accessed from everywhere. However, this procedure is absolutely bad practice, since it can very quickly lead to name conflicts (global scope pollution) that produce undesirable side effects. Edge Animate offers the option to set so-called symbol variables on the instance level of a symbol. The functions sym. `setVariable()` and sym `getVariable()` are available for this procedure. The exact signature of both functions is as follows:

```
// Set symbol variable
sym.setVariable( KEY, VALUE );

// Read symbol variable
var value = sym.getVariable( KEY );
```

The value to be set (VALUE) can be of any type; thus, you may use values such as integers, symbol instances, or arrays in this way:

```
// Set integer
sym.setVariable( "score", 123 );

// Set the symbol instance
sym.setVariable( "introSym", sym.getSymbol("intro") );

// Set array
sym.setVariable( "users", [user1, user2, user3] );
```

If you define (in the Library) a symbol that has individual parameters (that will be evaluated when an instance is created for the symbol that influences the display), symbol variables are always a good choice. Techniques such as how to set the display location of a map symbol in this manner are covered in section 7.3.

5.5.9   The sym Argument

Since nearly all actions use the `sym` argument of the enclosing function, it is important to understand this variable. It always returns a reference to the symbol of the currently open Timeline, which may initially seem a bit confusing when dealing with symbols. Suppose you have created a symbol and placed it on the Stage. This means you are still on the Timeline of the Stage itself. If you now add the `click` event to the symbol with a right-click and use the `sym` references within the action, it refers to the Stage itself and not the selected symbol.

Thus, the following action within a `click` event handler of a symbol starts playing its parent Timeline:

```
// Play parent Timeline (e.g. stage)
// of symbol
sym.play();
```

If you instead want to play the Timeline of the symbol itself, the action must be as follows:

```
// Play inner Timeline of symbol
sym.getSymbol("mySymbol").play();
```

5.6 Code Panels

So far you have only seen Edge Animate's actions Code panel. This window displays when you select Open Actions for XYZ from the right-click menu. This actions Code panel only affects the currently selected symbol. Use the + and - icons to add or remove actions for specific events.

Figure 5.20

The simple actions Code panel in Edge Animate

If you need to write a lot of actions and have to frequently switch back and forth between individual events or symbols, the program offers another Code panel for advanced users. This Code panel can be opened on the Windows menu:

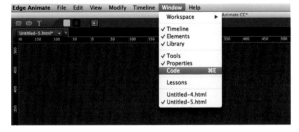

In Code view, you have access to all a composition's components. Thus, the left side displays the entire structure of the current composition (1). In this Code panel, you also use the + icon to add a new event. The advantages of this panel are pretty clear. You do not have to select the symbols or elements through multiple double-clicks, but you can use the search section to navigate directly to the right symbol or element (2). Like the actions Code panel, the right side of this panel contains the various actions code snippets (3). Additional features on the Code panel are the warnings at the bottom (4). This section alerts you to possible errors in the code, which is quite helpful for more complex code.

Figure 5.21

The full Code panel editor in Edge Animate provides significantly better navigation options

Furthermore, you can also switch to the Full Code view. While the normal view only displays the actions for the selected event, the Full Code view displays all actions data for your composition. Since you are working in the file level rather than the event level in this mode, the composition's components on the left are grayed out. This view should be used with caution. Only a few incorrect changes can make the entire composition useless, and Edge Animate needs a specific structure and comments to interpret the file. However, you are already well-versed in the file structure, or simply want to explore the structure of Edge Animate's actions files to better understand the JavaScript context for actions, this is the right panel to explore.

Figure 5.22

In the Code panel, you can view the entire JavaScript document for all actions with the Full Code view

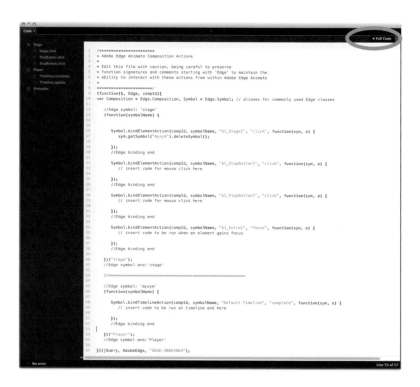

5.7   Edge Code and Brackets

If you want more ease of coding beyond Edge Animate's features, you should take a look at Brackets. This free and open-source code-editor is completely based on web standards, having been developed with HTML, CSS and JavaScript. The advantages are obvious: any web developer who uses Brackets to write JavaScript code is already able to customize the code-editor to his or her own needs. How this can look in everyday work is illustrated by the Brackets extension for the Edge Commons library, which I will introduce in section 7.4.

While the latest build of Brackets is available on the GitHub code-sharing website, Edge Code offers Adobe's own version of Brackets. The core of both versions is the same, but Edge Code contains a selection of pre-installed Adobe extensions, such as the use of font pools from Edge Web Fonts or the cloud services of PhoneGap Build.

Brackets and Edge Code are both strong supports for programming actions in Edge Animate. Since Edge Animate stores all project files as open HTML or JavaScript files during the design phase, you can simultaneously open a project in Edge Animate and Brackets / Edge Code. You can also use the many additional functions related to the writing of JavaScript code. However, since you work directly with the JavaScript file in these programs, you should only use Brackets / Edge Code if you have a sufficient level of expertise. If you have a project open simultaneously in Edge Animate and Brackets / Edge Code and make changes in the latter, when you return to Edge Animate, the program reminds you that the code has changed. You then have the choice to accept or reject the changes.

Figure 5.23

Brackets and Edge Code are the perfect additions when coding becomes more complex

📄 **Project**

The files for this example can be downloaded from http://edgebuch.simonwidjaja.com

Project Name: Interaction_Buttons

5.8　Lessons

In this chapter's sample project, you will learn how to create buttons with different states, and how to generate interval actions, which are independent from all Timelines, using `setInterval()`.

5.8.1　Buttons

Unlike Flash Professional, the first version of Edge Animate does not offer an infrastructure for multi-state buttons. However, we can use a small workaround to create multi-state buttons that can easily be reused. Let us first look at a simple button with only one state. Suppose we want to create a button that calls the website google.com when it is clicked.

1. Visual elements • First create a simple rectangle and a text field on the Stage.
2. Nesting • Because two separate elements are involved here, but we want to treat both levels as one button, we drag the text layer from the Elements panel onto the rectangle so that it has a child relationship to the shape. In this way, we ensure that all the settings, such as the mouse cursor and click events, apply to both elements, even if we only assign them to the parent rectangle.
3. Mouse cursor • Set the mouse cursor to pointer in the Property panel so that the user immediately recognizes our component as a button.
4. Action • To finish the task, add an action to call the URL for the `click` event. To do this, choose Open URL from the list of code snippets on the right, so that we only need to enter the intended URL. The button is now ready.

Figure 5.24

Four steps for creating a simple button

This will not work if you want to enhance your composition with multi-state buttons (e.g., mouseover and mousedown). The following example shows how to create a button template that you can reuse anytime by creating parameters for the text label. The finished composition with three buttons should look as follows:

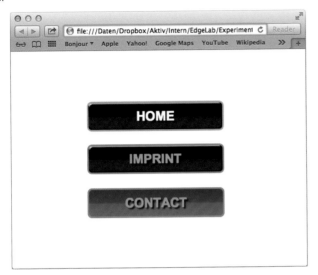

Figure 5.25
Three button component states with dynamic labels

1. Visual elements • For this step, follow your creative instincts and design a button. You can create elements out of basic shapes in Edge Animate as explained earlier, or with a graphics-editing program such as Photoshop or Fireworks. If you use a graphics-editing program, you should only create the background images for the individual states. The text box must be set in Edge Animate for each button; this is the only way it can be dynamically changed later. Place the graphics for all three states on the Stage so that they are perfectly aligned, one above the other.

2. Symbol • In the next step, select all components of the buttons and convert them to a symbol. This is then stored in the Library so it can later be placed on the Stage as often as needed. The name of the symbol is not important.

3. Defining the states • To define the states of the button, first go into the symbol by double-clicking it on the Stage or in the Library. Now create the states with keyframes on the Timeline within the symbol. To do this, set three labels. The first label is "normal" and is positioned at 0:00. The other two labels, "over," and "down," follow at intervals of one second. Modify the individual states of the labels by editing each of their levels.

Figure 5.26

The three labels for the states: normal, over, and down
The three jump labels for the states: normal, over, and down

4. Text label • To create a text label, simply add a text layer. We can adjust text properties such as color or shadow to match the button state as needed. It is only important that the text field be named "label" so that we can later set it dynamically.

5. Hotspot • Next, define a hotspot area that defines the action area of the button and listens to the events. To do this, add an arbitrary rectangle that is invisible (set opacity to 0). Name the rectangle "hotspot." In this way, only the text area is active. The symbol composition now appears as follows:

Figure 5.27
The visual appearance of the three button states

6. Mouse events • To display button states for the various mouse actions, set up four mouse events for the invisible hotspot level. For the `mousedown` event, the action that moves the Timeline is: `sym.stop("down");`. For the `mouseout` event, the action is: `sym.stop("normal");`. For the two events `mouseover` and `mouseup` the action is then: `sym.stop("over");`. If you drag several instances of the button from the Library onto the Stage and start the composition in the browser, you already see the buttons with the various states; however, these all have the same button text, so they are not really usable.

7. Enter the text label • Dynamic text fields present a small dilemma. We cannot define the actual text of each button in the symbol itself, since it would be inherited by all instances of the button, preventing the use of buttons with different texts in a composition. Besides symbols, Edge Animate does not offer any direct way to set values at the instance level. We could set the text label with symbol variables, but this is not particularly flexible, since we first have to give each button instance a name and then manually update all buttons in one action. This logic only affects the inner workings of the button, and should therefore remain encapsulated so that the user does not come in contact with the button symbols. For simple text labels, Edge Animate offers a workaround that is perfect for our project. Use the Accessibility section in the Property panel to set the button text. When you define the text label in the Title field for each button instance, you can get them within the symbol definition and assign them to the text fields created earlier.

Figure 5.28
Use the Title field in the Accessibility section to create dynamic text labels

8. Setting the text label with an action • To filter the set text within the symbol, create an action for the `creationComplete` event inside the symbol. This is always fired when a new instance of the button is created on the Stage during runtime. Now we can use the previously set text that has only been saved as a simple `title` attribute in the HTML tag, and assign it to the text field using the `html()` function:

```
// Read title attribute and use it as label
var title = sym.getSymbolElement().attr( "title" );
sym.$( "label" ).html( title );
```

5.8.2   Interval Updates Without Timeline (Edge Clock)

Often you will want actions to perform continuously at a defined interval. This can be useful if animations repeat or if data is requested from an outside web service, such as for Twitter feeds, after a certain time window. You have many different events available for which you can write handlers to trigger the actions; however, since all events in Edge Animate are either linked to active user interaction or the Timeline itself, there is no guarantee that the action will be regularly executed. The `update` event of the Timeline is probably the most obvious event for implementing such a scenario. The only catch is that the Timeline must be actually played so that the event is run. If you pause the Timeline on which the event is registered, the event will not execute. However, since we are working with JavaScript, as soon as we start to place code in Edge Animate, we have the full functionality of JavaScript available. We can use the global function `setInterval()` to define another function that should execute in a user-defined interval—and one that is not dependent on the state of the Timeline.

The following example illustrates the use of an interval through an Edge clock that displays the current time using three bars. The lengths of the bars represent hours, minutes, and seconds, respectively. We will use an image that was previously created in Photoshop.

Figure 5.29
Using the JavaScript interval, repetitive actions can be executed independently of the Timeline

1. New Edge Animate project • First create a new Edge Animate project as usual and name it "Edge Clock." The supplied background image is 740 px wide and 400 px high. Set the dimensions of the Stage in Edge Animate so that the background image fills the entire composition.

2. Create bars • Next, create the three bars to display the hours, minutes, and seconds. To have the bars exactly fit into the rounded area, use the Rounded Rectangle Tool to create rectangles with rounded corners. Select this tool from the top Tools panel and draw a rectangle on the Stage. Assign the shape with a width of 400 px and a height of 16 px. After you have given the bar any fill color, work on the rounded corners. Since all corners should look the same, select "1" in the Corners section on the Property panel for rounded corners. Now enter the value "12" next to the grid square below to set the rounding for all four corners simultaneously. Since we need a total of three bars, duplicate the bar twice with the Edit menu, selecting Duplicate. Since we will later want to address each of the bars in our script, it helps to give them each unique, identifying names. Use the following names in descending order to name the bars: hoursBar, minutesBar, and secondsBar. Now the bars will be stored under the defined names as DIV containers in the DOM, to be accessed later.

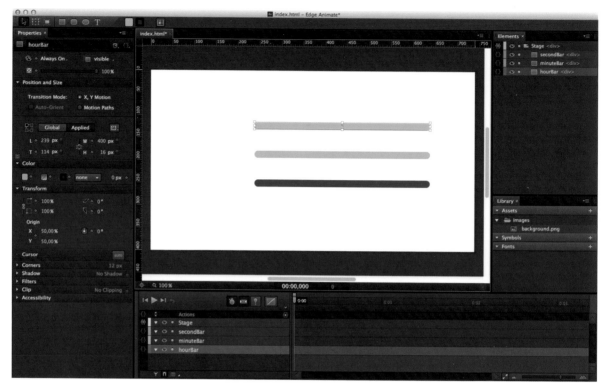

Figure 5.30
Three bars with rounded corners for
hours, minutes, and seconds

3. Add background • Next, import your preferred background by simply dragging it from the computer's file system directly onto the Stage. Since you
want this image to appear behind the bar you created earlier, you must
make sure it is defined in the DOM before the bars. You can check this in the
Elements panel and correct it if necessary. Make sure that the background
image is at the very bottom of the hierarchy so that it is the first element to
be defined in the DOM.

Figure 5.31
A simple PNG image as the background
for the Edge Clock

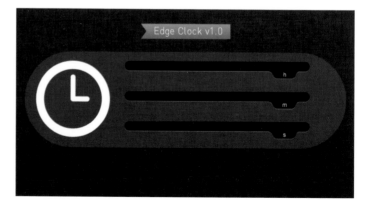

4. Adjust the placement of the bars on the background • Position the bars on the Stage so that they fit into the lighter grey area on the background image. Since the fixed coordinates in CSS are always at the top left edge of the element, this position will be retained, even when we dynamically adjust the width of the element via script in the next step. In this way, the timing information can be altered to fit the width of the bar via a simple conversion.

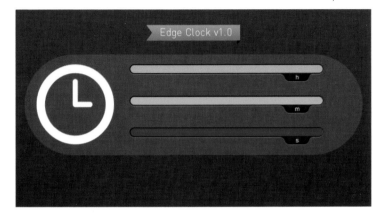

Figure 5.32
Background image with bars

5. Initializing interval at startup • Since the visual surface of the clock is ready, you can now turn to its inner workings. First, consider when the interval should be started. One possibility is an activation switch. In this example, however, it should start up right at the beginning of the composition. This is best done with the compositionReady event because it is fired once, as soon as the composition is fully displayed. Click the Open Actions icon next to the composition name and make sure that no elements have been selected on the Stage. Now add the compositionReady event and fill it in with the following script to initialize the interval:

```
// Register Interval
setInterval(update, 1000);

// Function to be called per interval
function update() {
    // Code to update Bars
}
```

6. Interval Logic • The setInterval() method takes two parameters. The first is the name of the function that will be regularly called. Make sure that you pass a reference to the function by using parentheses to avoid calling the function. The time is given in milliseconds so that the 1.000 value is ideal for the second-by-second call. Next, implement the code to determine the time and adjust the bars. For this, extend the update() method as follows:

```
// Register Interval
setInterval(update, 1000);

// Function to be called per interval
function update() {
    try {
        // Get Date
        var currentDate = new Date();
        var hoursInPixel = currentDate.getHours()
            *(400/24) + "px";
        var minutesInPixel = currentDate.getMinutes()
            *(400/60) + "px";
        var secondsInPixel = currentDate.getSeconds()
            *(400/60) + "px";

        // Update Hours
        var hourBar = sym.$("hourBar");
        hourBar.css( "width", hoursInPixel );

        // Update Minutes
        var minuteBar = sym.$("minuteBar");
        minuteBar.css( "width", minutesInPixel );

        // Update Seconds
        var secondBar = sym.$("secondBar");
        secondBar.css( "width", secondsInPixel );
} catch (error) {
    console.log("Error: ", error);
}
}
```

7. Time calculation • As you can see, we create a time object with the current time using `new Date()`. We use `getHours()`, `getMinutes()` and `getSeconds()` to get the values we want and translate these into pixels that fit our bar width. To assign the new width to the bar, first obtain a reference to it. To do this, we use the $ symbol provided by the jQuery function. As selector, pass it the name of the element as a string. Now that we have this reference, use the width value of the `css()` method to set the width of the element. Repeat this for all three bars, and violà: the clock is ready.

In this example, you learned how to execute actions in a user-defined interval without playback on the Timeline. Other possible useful scenarios for intervals are:

▶ Get current tweets from Twitter
▶ Monitor user activity (e.g., mouse movement)
▶ Check if the window is in the browser's focus

Of course, you can stop such an interval again at any time. For this, use the `clearInterval (intervalId)` method as follows:

```
// Start interval
var refreshIntervalId = setInterval( fname, 10000 );
// Stop interval
clearInterval( refreshIntervalId );
```

Publishing

6   Publishing

In this chapter, we will cover how to publish completed Edge Animate compositions. Since Edge Animate saves all project data with web standards compatibility during animation design, these files can easily be placed on a web server through methods such as FTP file transfer and made available on a domain. This method is entirely suitable for internal approval processes or presentations. However, if you want to use your compositions live online in a productive manner, such a method is not appropriate. The project files from Edge Animate first need to be optimized for their file size. The following pages will cover how to carry out such an optimization process and how to use Preloaders in Edge Animate. Also, you will learn how to use a poster for older browsers in a Down-level Stage. In the lessons section, we will look at publishing with the WordPress blogging system, and integration in digital publications with InDesign.

6.1   Preparations

> ✎ **Down-level Stage**
> A simplified version of the Stage with reduced functionality so that it can easily display in older browsers.

Edge Animate provides functions to deal with the technical differences that may occur when your composition is viewed on different browsers. For example, you can use a poster of your composition on a limited stage without animations for display in older browsers, or you can define a Preloader that updates the user on the loading process in instances of a slow Internet connection or large composition data size.

6.1.1   Posters

Since Edge Animate compositions cannot be shown on older browsers (earlier than IE 9), you need to make provisions. Edge Animate enables you to create what is known as a Down-level Stage. In most instances, the Down-level Stage is really just a scaled-back image, a kind of screen shot that contains the composition's most relevant contents. In this way, users with older browsers see at least the main message of an advertising campaign and are not excluded from whatever the animation is trying to communicate. Such posters are very easy to create in Edge Animate; you do not have to take a screenshot manually and then edit it to work as a static image. First, you need to be on the Stage to create a poster. The Property panel on the left contains a section called Poster. Click the camera icon, and a dialog box opens in which you can create a static image (2) from the current location of the playhead on the Timeline (1). The dialog box lets you either capture a new poster image or refresh a prior one. The poster is saved as a PNG image in your project images subfolder.

Figure 6.1
Capture a poster image or refresh a
previously created poster

Once the poster is created and added to the Library, you can use it in various
scenarios. Some publishing options, such as the use of Edge Animate compositions in InDesign, use posters to represent Edge Animate compositions before
they are fully launched. To change these settings, the second Poster dialog box
gives you direct access to the Publish Settings dialog box. If you are strictly publishing on the web, posters are only used in the Down-level Stage. If you want to
use the created Poster on the Internet, click the Edit Down-level Stage button to
navigate to the alternate Stage.

> **✎ InDesign with DPS**
> The Adobe Digital Publishing Suite
> (DPS) uses the familiar InDesign
> page layout program to create
> digital and interactive publications
> for tablets. It enables the integration
> of content based on open web
> standards.

6.1.2   Down-Level Stage

You can either navigate to the Down-level Stage through the above-mentioned dialog box for creating poster images or via the Edit button in the Down-level Stage section of the Property panel. Once you are in the Down-level Stage, Edge Animate's scope of functions is immediately reduced to the functions supported in older browsers. For example, the Timeline is entirely deactivated and grayed out(1). The Stage itself still looks the same (2), but even here, functionality is very limited. For example, you can no longer group elements or convert them to symbols. The Property panel (3) on the left side only gives you the option of adding the Poster that you created earlier.

Figure 6.2

The Down-level Stage with reduced functionality

In addition to graphics and images from the Library, text elements can be placed on this reduced Stage. For such text elements, you can set basic text formatting properties (1) as well as a target URL (2). The hyperlink is the only interaction possible in this mode.

6.1.3 Preloader

Since Edge Animate compositions can have a large data size (it is easy to quickly reach 300 kB–500 kB), Edge Animate offers the capability to create a simple Preloader for display until the composition is fully loaded. Edge Animate offers two different types of Preloaders: *immediate* and *polite*. Both are very similar in behavior except for one point: the *immediate* option attempts to immediately load all assets required by the composition. The *polite* option waits for the HTML document's onload event to occur before loading the assets. The latter option can be useful for compositions with a large data volume because the loading of the page's other static content isn't blocked.

Figure 6.3
Two types of Preloaders: *immediate* and *polite*

Use the Edit button in the Preloader section of the Property panel to make changes to the Preloader. Here again, you have access to a Stage with very limited functionality.

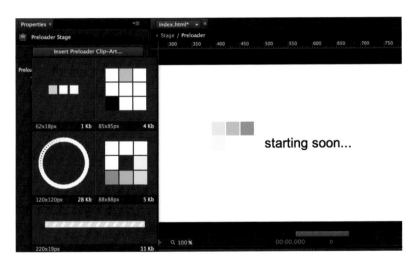

Figure 6.4
Edge Animate offers several Preloader templates

Figure 6.5

Figure 6.5
When creating a Preloader, you should
pay particular attention to the data
volume

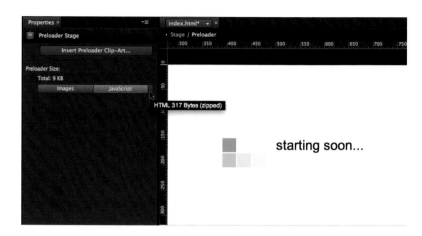

Just like with the Down-level Stage, you only use text, graphics, and images from the Library. Be careful to only use visual elements that have a very small file size. Requiring a Preloader to display large amounts of data is absurd since its purpose is to show viewers when the real data is finally loaded. In addition, the dialog box offers a few predefined Preloader animations with data sizes between 1 kb and 29 kb. You can place these anywhere on the Stage to inform the user of the loading procedure. However, the animation runs in a simple loop (animated GIF), thus providing no information on the actual loading progress.

A Preloader should be as minimalistic as possible and you must constantly monitor the file size needed to play it. For that reason, Edge Animate displays a simple graphic that indicates the actual image size, JavaScript size, and HTML size.

6.2   Export and Settings

Since compositions created in Edge Animate can be used in different scenarios, the program offers a number of different export or publishing profiles. Use the Menu File > Publish Settings to select and configure different profiles. All profiles store the final export files in the publish subfolder of your project directory.

6.2.1   Web Profile

Use the first Web profile if your composition is to be loaded and displayed in a browser. This profile minimizes file sizes and optimizes performance for all HTML and JavaScript elements. The dialog box lets you define the default output folder and set three more options. The Google Chrome Frame option is used for displaying Edge Animate content in older versions of Internet Explorer (6–8).

In addition, you can opt to deliver the frameworks used in your composition (jQuery, Edge Animate, etc.) via an alternate content delivery network (CDN). This means that the generic elements of your composition are not pulled from your own server but from a central system, such as Google CDN. CDN enables frameworks to cache better, which results in a significantly shorter loading time. However, this option only works if an Internet connection exists. If a composition must also run offline, you should not use this option. The third control option writes your animation content into the HTML document rather than adding all the elements at runtime through JavaScript. This can have several advantages. Firstly, this option makes your content more accessible to search engines. With static HTML, you do not have to wait for an event before you can access individual elements using external frameworks.

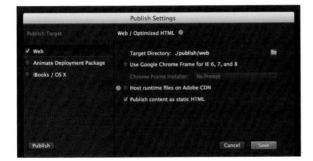

Figure 6.6
Publishing options for the web

Saving an Edge Animate project immediately generates all JavaScript files, including the corresponding An file type. The selection of files below shows which ones are actually needed to run the composition, making them essential to the functioning of the animation. The An project file is only used to open the project in Edge Animate, and only contains data for the actual design. You can already upload the selected files to any web server.

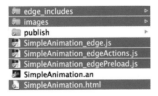

However, because these files are not yet optimized, you should use Edge Animate's publishing feature, instead. The publish/web folder only contains relevant files after a successful export. These are optimized for the web and can be immediately put online.

Figure 6.7
The file structure after publishing
for the web

The files in the first level, along with the `images` folder, are the project-specific files, whereas the `edge_includes` folder contains the generic JavaScript libraries that are identical for each project. This means that multiple compositions could use the same `edge_includes` folder in practice.

6.2.2   Animate Deployment Package Profile

The second profile packs the entire composition into a single file that can be used for integration with other Adobe tools. This deployment package carries the file extension `*.oam` and can currently be imported into Dreamweaver, Muse, and InDesign. Moreover, this export option is also used for third-party websites, similar to the CMS plug-in Edge Suite for Wordpress and Drupal. An oam file is technically nothing more than a ZIP archive that contains all project files and additional XML data for the import and export functions.

Figure 6.8
The Animate Deployment Package
Export format for integration with other
Adobe products

6.2.3 iBooks / OS X Profile

The third publishing profile, iBooks / oS X, creates a widget that can be used in two ways. Firstly, the exported `wdgt` files can be used in Apple's authoring tool, iBooks Author, as an enhancement to multi-touch books. Moreover, widgets exported with this setting can be added to the dashboard on the OS X operating system. The latter is a nice side effect that enables you to produce at least simple desktop applications with Edge Animate. Since Windows 8 increasingly relies on the use of web standards for desktop applications, the integration of Edge Animate compositions on the Windows desktop will likely be possible in the near future.

> **✎ iBooks / OS X**
> Please note that this profile does not allow the use of GIF files.

Figure 6.9
Edge Animate compositions can also be used in Apple's iBooks Author

6.3 Lessons

6.3.1 Publishing Compositions With FTP

If you want to publish a stand-alone composition on the web, it is best to upload the files from the `publish/web` folder described above, using FTP (File Transfer Protocol). You can use any web server, since Edge Animate compositions consist exclusively of static HTML and JavaScript files and must be uploaded without additional server logic. If an animation is supposed to run directly on a domain or a folder without specifying the actual file name, you can rename the primary HTML file of your project (e.g. `SimpleAnimation.html` to `index.html`).

📑 Project

The files for this example can be downloaded from http://edgebuch. simonwidjaja.com

Project Name: Publishing_Embed

6.3.2 Embedding Compositions in an HTML Website

It rarely happens that an Edge Animate composition is published as a stand-alone. Animations are usually integrated into online websites. This can be done in several ways. You can use the `object` or `iframe` tag to place the entire Edge Animate-generated HTML page into an existing HTML document. This option is advantageous because the existing document only needs extensions in one place, and the document's DOM does not have to be directly appended with the many DOM elements of your composition. This produces a clean encapsulation of the animation. A program such as Dreamweaver can be used when using this option to place an Edge Animate composition. The following example assumes that the Edge Animate composition called "Simple Animation" is published from the "edge" subfolder of the existing website.

```
<!doctype html>
<html>
<head><!-- ... --></head>
<body>
      <div id="page">
      <h1>Edge Animate Composition</h1>
       <!--Composition-->
       <object id="EdgeID" name="EdgeID"
         type="text/html"
         width="1000" height="320"
         data="edge/SimpleAnimation.html">
         </object>
      </div>
</body>
</html>
```

If you do not want this type of encapsulation, such as when you need communication between individual elements or across the entire composition, you can directly integrate the composition in the DOM of the current HTML document. To do this, look at the HTML file generated by Edge Animate to see how to insert the created composition in HTML. Basically, two elements are required to play a composition: a DIV container must be placed in the document's body section as the Stage (1). Moreover, `XXX_edgePreload.js` must be loaded into the document's head section (2) so that all dependent files are loaded when the website is called. This then writes the DOM elements of the composition in the DIV container that was created earlier.

```
<!doctype html>
<html>
<head>
<!-- ... -->
```

```
<!--Adobe Edge Runtime (2)-->
    <script type="text/javascript« charset="utf-8"
        src="SimpleAnimation_edgePreload.js"></script>
    <style>
        .edgeLoad-EDGE-535631250 { visibility:hidden; }
    </style>
<!--Adobe Edge Runtime End-->
</head>
<body>
    <div id="page">
        <h1>Edge Animate Composition (DOM)</h1>
        <!--Container for Composition (1)-->
        <div id="Stage" class="EDGE-535631250"></div>
    </div>
</body>
</html>
```

Both options can also be used to embed several compositions within an HTML document.

6.3.3 Edge Animate and DPS

Frequently, Edge Animate compositions are used in web content management systems (WCMS). Compositions can be integrated into content pages or page templates on the code level, as previously described. Since the strength of a WCMS is the significant simplification of additions or modification of text and media files through a user interface, there are already preliminary attempts to offer this functionality for Edge Animate compositions. Under the *Edge Commons—Dirty Little Helpers for Edge Animate*, my colleague, Timm Jansen, has developed two plug-ins/modules that make publishing Edge Animate compositions in the WordPress and Drupal systems astoundingly easy. The modules not only allow the use of any number of compositions on your website, they also take over all file handling.

I will only be discussing the highly popular WordPress blog system here; however, http://www.edgedocs.com/edgecommons has more information on the Drupal module, which, at the time of writing, was already better than WordPress in terms of functionality. For example, the Data Injection feature is already supported in Drupal, which allows the injection of dynamic data into compositions.

Let's take a closer look at the workflow with Edge Animate and WordPress. The aim of this sample project is to use an Edge Animate composition to enhance a simple post on a newly created Wordpress blog. This is easy to do since both elements are completely based on web standards, and all functions (interactivity, etc.) in our Edge Animate composition are maintained. The final result should look as follows:

> **WCMS**
> Web content management systems are software for community creation, editing, and organizing of content on a website. A basic principle of WCMS is the strict separation of content, design, and function.

> **Project**
> The files for this example can be downloaded from http://edgebuch.simonwidjaja.com
> **Project Name:** Publishing_CMS

Figure 6.10

An Edge Animate composition in the
WordPress blog system

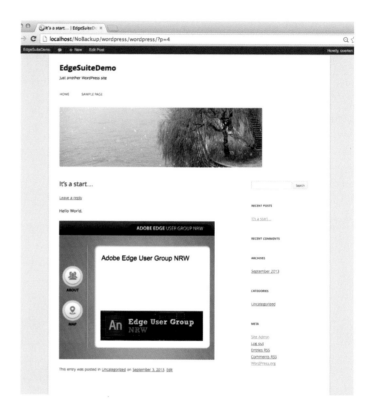

1. Install plug-in • Before working on the Edge Animate page, first prepare Wordpress. Use the WordPress infrastructure to install the plug-in. Select the Plugins menu item from your page's Administration screen. You can search the many plug-ins listed under the Install menu item. Enter "Edge Suite" as a search term and then click Install Now when the plug-in is located.

Figure 6.11

This WordPress plug-in Edge Suite can
be installed directly on the WordPress
interface

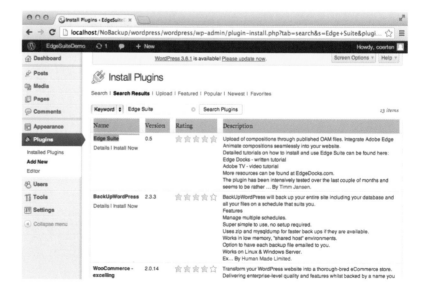

2. Edge Animate Composition • This displays a new menu item on the left side of the Administration screen, and the preparations are now complete. Now you can load any compositions on the page. Since Edge Animate compositions consist of many files and folders that are only partially suitable for upload, the WordPress plug-in Animate Package will help you in this process. Open the composition in Edge Animate, select Animate Deployment Package in the Publishing Settings as pictured below, and click Publish:

Figure 6.12
The Animate Deployment Package is used to publish in WordPress

3. Locate File • After we published our composition, we see the new `animate package` folder in the publish folder that contains the zipped composition in the oam file format. The WordPress plug-in supports exactly this data type.

Figure 6.13
The exported Animate Deployment Package (`*.oam`) for use in WordPress

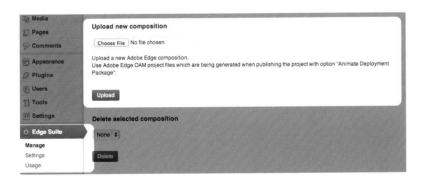

Figure 6.14
Website compositions can be added in the Manage section of the Edge Suite plug-ins for global use on the website

4. Upload • Back in WordPress, Select the Edge Suite menu item. In the upload dialog, select and upload the previously published composition.

5. Shortcode • The composition has now been added to the file structure of your WordPress site. There are several possibilities for positioning the composition. In this example, we are restricting ourselves to publishing compositions in content fields. The plug-in relies on the usual shortcodes for this use case. To enable this feature, first choose the Settings menu item, and then activate the Widget Shortcode checkbox. You can now use shortcodes in any content fields for the published composition.

Figure 6.15
To use compositions within an article, the Widget Shortcode option must be enabled

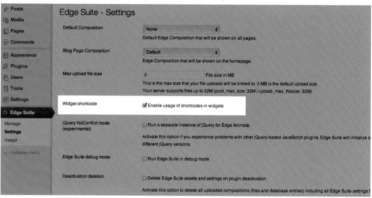

6. Composition number • Since the shortcodes require the composition number, we first have to determine it. Call up the Manage subpage again to view all the composition numbers of all published compositions in the Delete section. For this example, the composition uses the number 3.

7. Place composition • We now have all the necessary information to place the composition in the blog post. Edit the post and place the shortcode `[edge_animation id="3"]` at the correct place in the text box. After saving, you can see the composition on the finished page.

Figure 6.16
The WordPress shortcodes to insert a
composition within an article

6.3.4 InDesign (DPS)

The Digital Publishing Suite (DPS) can be used to create digital and interactive publications for tablets. The DPS is an integral component of InDesign, and also supports HTML content for the enhancement of interactive publications. Because Edge Animate uses HTML and related web standards, it is a short bridge between both creative tools. For any digital publishing project, InDesign supports the import of Edge Animate compositions. This process also relies on the Animate Deployment Package that was already presented in the section on WordPress. Since the Digital Publishing Suite is a rather complex issue, the following sample project will focus on just the essentials. We will use the DPS to create a small, interactive publication that will contain a full-screen animation on the second page. For the sake of simplicity, we will use the iPad2 as target platform here. Of course, DPS also supports other platforms, such as Android.

1. Edge Animate Composition • In this example, we will create an interactive publication in landscape format for the iPad 2. Start by creating a new composition with the dimensions 1024 x 768 px. For the animation, import images that you will animate as usual on the Timeline, and add any interactions of your choice. In the final publications on the iPad, a WebKit instance is used for rendering HTML content and your animation. Consequently, the composition behaves just like it would in the browser and you have use of the entire scope of functions. For user interaction, use the touch event rather than the `click` event, since these are specifically optimized for touch surfaces, such as the iPad, and react much faster and more accurately. Save the finished composition in the Publish Settings dialog as an `oam` Deployment Package so that you can import it into InDesign.

> ✎ **Alternative Layouts**
>
> Starting with InDesign CS6, besides fixed page dimensions that apply to an entire project, you will also be able to create so-called alternative layouts, which depict the same contents in customized layouts for different output sizes. This makes it possible to display the publications on different devices.

2. Creating a DPS project in InDesign • In InDesign, create a new document in the program's standard dialog. Set the document's intent to Digital Publishing so that the proper tools, such as Folio Overlays, etc., are displayed in the project. Choose the iPad as a primary target device, and set the desired number of pages.

Figure 6.17
Creating a new DPS project in InDesign

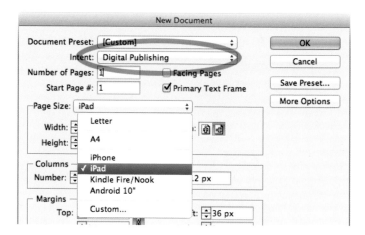

3. Importing the composition • Once the project is created, you can start with the layout of each page and place content. On the first page, place dummy text for the later demonstration of the different pages. Scroll to the second page and place the previously created Edge Animate composition: either place the oam file via the Place dialog, or drag the file directly from Explorer or Finder into InDesign.

Figure 6.18
An Edge Animate composition embedded in a DPS article

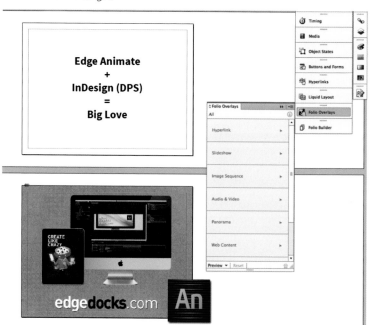

4. Create folio • The article is now ready for interactive publication. A folio, which is how publications are referred to in DPS, consists of at least one article. In order to test the article, create a new folio by clicking on the Create Folio icon in the Folio Builder. Set the dimensions and orientation of the folio in the dialog box that opens. In the next step, add the open document to the folio as an article.

5. Testing and exporting • Once the publication has been completed, you can test it and publish it via Adobe's infrastructure in the various online stores. Use the Preview button on the Folio Builder tab to test the publication on the desktop in the Adobe Content Viewer, or use the Adobe server infrastructure to test your publication on your test device.

For Advanced Users

7   For Advanced Users

Now that you understand all the important basics of Edge Animate, it's time to take a closer look at the extensibility of your compositions. As already mentioned, Edge Animate runtime is largely based on the popular jQuery JavaScript framework. Starting in 2012, my colleagues, Johannes Boyne and Timm Jansen, and I used this knowledge as a starting point to explore the long-term potential of Edge Animate, particularly in terms of integration into external systems and extensibility with additional frameworks and custom components. The results have been incorporated into my open source library, Edge Commons, and they form the basis for additional functions such as logging, parallax, sound, and data injection. However, before we look at the Edge Commons in detail, I want to outline the basics on how to extend Edge Animate compositions so that you can develop your own components.

7.1   External Components

Through the use of jQuery, we can load any external HTML and JavaScript components, and place them in our composition. Let us first look at how to load external libraries.

7.1.1   yepnope.js

Because an Edge Animate composition is made up of several components, the library loader yepnope.js is used in Edge Animate runtime. This loader makes it very easy to create conditions that can be used for loading different JavaScript or CSS files. If you want to write your own instructions for loading external libraries or style sheets, you can use yepnope.js.

Suppose you want to load an external JavaScript file at runtime. This can be done with the following line of code:

```
yepnope({load: "http://URL/script.js"});
```

This statement loads the `script.js` file, adds it to the DOM of the current page, and then executes it. Since this operation runs asynchronously rather than directly (in other words, it only completes after a certain time delay), you cannot access the contents of the script in the line immediately after the statement. Therefore, the following extended yepnope function is often used, in which a function is passed as a so-called callback. This callback function is executed internally by yepnope.js as soon as the requested file is completely loaded. This ensures that the content is not accessed too early, avoiding a potential error.

```
yepnope({
    load: "http://URL/script.js"
    callback: function() {
        // File fully loaded
    }
});
```

Moreover, yepnope.js is able to load multiple files with a single command. To do this, you can use the `both` parameter and pass an array with the files you want to load. The callback function will be executed only when all of the requested files have been loaded.

```
yepnope({
    both: [
        "http://URL/script.js",
        "http://URL/styles.css"
    ],
    callback: function() {
        // File fully loaded
    }
});
```

More specific examples of how to use yepnope.js in Edge Animate are presented in sections 7.1.4 and 7.4.

7.1.2 Google Maps

Before we look at more complex extensions, let's start with simple external services that offer embedding functions through iframes. Google Maps is used in many projects as a simple location description and offers an iframe option on the website for such purposes:

Figure 7.1

Obtaining the embed code from Google Maps

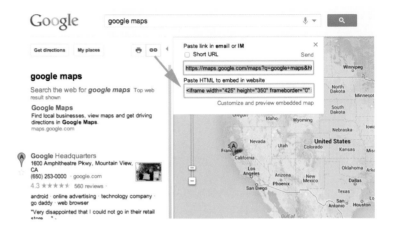

We cannot simply copy this embed code in the HTML document of our Edge Animate project because we want to define the exact place for the map within Edge Animate. To do this, create a simple rectangle in Edge Animate and name it `"container."` This rectangle is represented as a DIV container in the DOM; now we can inject the embed code into that DIV container using jQuery.

Figure 7.2

The container and the final maps component in Edge Animate

 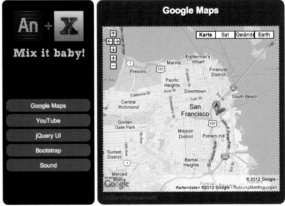

Now that we have obtained a reference to the target container using jQuery and put the iframe code in a variable, we can add the HTML snippet for the iframe to the container with `container.html(map)`. The final script for injecting the code can be used in the event `compositionReady`, for example, and looks as follows:

```
var container = sym.$("container");
var map = '<iframe width="'+container.width()+'"
   height="'+container.height()+'" frameborder="0"
   scrolling="no" marginheight="0" marginwidth="0"
   src="http://maps.google.de/maps?ie=UTF8&amp;q=adobe
   +san+francisco&amp;fb=1&amp;gl=de&amp;hq=adobe&
   amp;hnear=0x80859a6d00690021:0x4a501367f076adff,San+
   Francisco,+California+United+States&amp;c
   id=0,0,7657507985557832261&amp;ll=37.771401,-
   122.401989&amp;spn=0.006295,0.006295&amp;t=m&amp;iwlo
   c=A&amp;output=embed"></iframe>';
container.html( map );
```

In this example, the iframe code was slightly modified so that the loaded map exactly fit the target container. To do this, the static values for `width` and `height` were replaced by the `container.width()` and `container.height()` values.

7.1.3 Videos (YouTube)

The iframe option is widely used. You can also use it to integrate videos from platforms like YouTube:

```
var container = sym.$("container");
var youtube = '<iframe width="'+container.width()+'"
   height="'+container.height()+'" src="http://www.you
   tube.com/embed/CBF92LoXziU" frameborder="0" allow
   fullscreen></iframe>';
container.html(youtube);
```

Here again, the size of the iframe, and thus the actual video, is adapted to fit the container. If you want to use an overlay in which the video appears, you should look at the Spotlight feature of Edge Commons in section 7.4.3.

> ✎ **jQuery UI**
> jQuery UI offers numerous application components such as accordions, buttons, dialogs, menus, and various input components. The jQuery UI requires jQuery.

Figure 7.3
jQuery UI offers a variety of components.
You can try them out on the jqueryui.
com website.

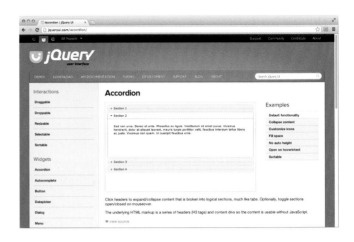

7.1.4   jQuery UI Components

Many projects require more complex data entry components for forms or other features. Since the first version of Edge Animate does not offer any components of this type, we have to rely on external component libraries. Since Edge Animate already includes the jQuery framework, look for the extension in the jQuery UI components to keep the overall composition as lean as possible. The following example shows the use of jQuery UI in an Edge Animate composition. First off, two containers are created and filled via the `html()` method with a simple text input field. The second one is also assigned an additional unique ID. The yepnope function outlined above is used to load the minified version of the jQuery UI and its style sheet. In this example, we are assuming that both files were previously downloaded from the jQuery UI website and have been stored in the `libs` folder of our Edge Animate project. Alternatively, you can also use online versions of the jQuery CDN server (http://code.jquery.com/). Once both files have been loaded, the text box with the `datepicker ID` created earlier is converted into an input field for a date with the jQuery statement `$("# datepicker"). datepicker()`. The final code looks as follows and can be used, for example, in the `compositionReady` event of the composition:

```
// Simple Input (1)
var ex1 = sym.$( "example1" );
ex1.html( '<input type="text" />' );
// Datepicker (2)
var ex2 = sym.$( "example2" );
ex2.html( '<input type="text« id="datepicker" />' );

// Load jQuery
yepnope({
    both: [
```

```
        "libs/jquery-ui.min.js",
        "libs/jquery-ui.css"
    ],
    callback: function(){
        $( "#datepicker" ).datepicker();
    }
});
```

The result in the browser looks as follows: (1) is the conventional text entry field, and (2) is how it looks with the jQuery UI extension.

Figure 7.4

The date picker jQuery UI component in the Edge Animate composition

7.2 Wiring Multiple Compositions on One Page

Of course, you can also use several compositions in one HTML document. To do this, make sure that the composition files can be correctly accessed by the HTML document, and that the blocks of script and the Stage DIV containers are placed in the body segment of the HTML document. This can be done with any number of components. To enable communication between the individual compositions, the Edge Animate runtime provides a special bootstrap method. This method is necessary because, for example, the Timeline control of a composition will require a reference to it. Since the compositions are loaded asynchronously, there is no guarantee, for example, that in a compositionReady event of a composition, the loading of another composition has already been completed.

The following example illustrates the use of the bootstrap method using two compositions. The red composition, CompositionA, runs a simple animation on the main Timeline, but is not automatically played. The second composition, in green, contains a simple button that, when clicked, starts the animation in the red composition.

Figure 7.5

Communication between compositions
with bootstrap callback

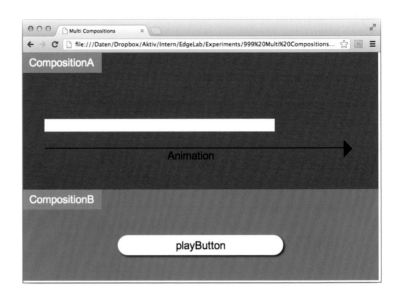

▤ Project

The files for this example can be
downloaded from http://edgebuch.
simonwidjaja.com

Project Name:
Advanced_Multi_Compositions

After creating both compositions in Edge Animate and storing them in the
same folder, create a new HTML document (e.g., index.html) with the two compositions as follows:

```html
<!DOCTYPE html>
<html>
<head>
    <meta .../>
    <title>Multi Compositions</title>

<!--Adobe Edge Runtime-->
    <script type="text/javascript" charset="utf-8"
        src="CompositionA_edgePreload.js"></script>
    <style>
        .edgeLoad-COMPOSITION_A {visibility:hidden; }
    </style>
<!--Adobe Edge Runtime End-->

<!--Adobe Edge Runtime-->
    <script type="text/javascript" charset="utf-8"
        src="CompositionB_edgePreload.js"></script>
```

```
    <style>
        .edgeLoad-COMPOSITION_B { visibility:hidden; }
    </style>
<!--Adobe Edge Runtime End-->

</head>
<body style="margin:0;padding:0;">

    <div id="Stage" class="COMPOSITION_A"></div>
    <div id="StageB" class="COMPOSITION_B"></div>
</body>
</html>
```

In this method, make sure to change the IDs of the DIV container for the two stages. You may use any name, but it must be unique and can only be used once within the document. As described above, direct access to CompositionA within CompositionB would likely not produce any results and cause an error because there is no guarantee that CompositionA is already fully loaded when the function is called. This is where the bootstrap callback, which you can define with `Adobe Edge.bootstrapCallback()`, comes into play. For this purpose, first create a new script block in the head segment of the HTML document. In this script block, define an empty object named `loadedComps` in which you can later store the references to the compositions. In the second step, define the actual bootstrap callback by creating a function with the parameter `compId`. This function is executed every time a composition is loaded in the document. In this example, the callback will be called twice in a row. Since we cannot predict which composition is loaded first, save the composition that has just loaded in the `loadedComps` object. The following if statement checks whether both compositions are available. If this is not the case, then nothing happens and there is a wait for the next composition. Once both compositions are available, register an action for the button inside the green composition. To do this, use the `bindElement()` function. Within the action, you get the reference to CompositionA. Use the `play()` function on the Stage so that the animation is played. The final script block looks as follows.

```
<script>
    var loadedComps = {};
    AdobeEdge.bootstrapCallback( function(compId) {
        loadedComps[compId] = AdobeEdge.
            getComposition(compId);
        if (loadedComps['COMPOSITION_A']
            && loadedComps['COMPOSITION_B']) {
            AdobeEdge.Symbol.bindElementAction(compId,
                "stage", "${_playButton}", "click",
```

```
function(sym, e) {
    loadedComps["COMPOSITION_A"].getStage()
    .play();
});
    }
});
</script>
```

Figure 7.6

The basic structure of a reusable
component

7.3   Reusable Components

Since Edge Animate supports the export and import of symbols, you can easily create reusable components for use in various projects. In a simple export,
the symbol can only be imported in an identical form into other projects, so
you should consider whether it makes sense to set parameters for the individual properties. In this way, you can customize the symbol to suit your target
project. The following example shows a Google Maps component with a visible
container and title. The component will be used so that both the title and the
displayed location within the map are externally defined, such as by the parent
composition in the target project.

For this purpose, we create the visual elements as shown in the figure here,
and then convert it all into a new symbol. Inside the symbol, we make the individual components visible on the symbol Timeline. Once everything is visible,
we set a trigger with the following script:

```
try {
    //---------------
    // Parameters
    //---------------
    var title = sym.getVariable("title");
    if (!title) { console.warn("MapContainer: Please set
        variable 'title'"); return; }
    var map = sym.getVariable("map");
    if (!map) { console.warn("MapContainer: Please
        set variable 'map'"); return; }

    //---------------
    // Creation
    //---------------
    // title
    sym.$("title").html(title);
    // map
    var mapContainer = sym.$("mapContainer");
    map = map.replace(/width="[0-9]*"/,
        'width="'+mapContainer.width()+'"');
    map = map.replace(/height="[0-9]*"/,
        'height="'+mapContainer.height()+'"');
    mapContainer.html(map);
}
catch (error) {
    if (console && console.error) {
        console.error("Error: ", error.toString());
    }
}
```

In the Parameters section, we first get the symbol variables `title` and `map`. Since both parameters are compulsory, we query the values to output an error, when necessary.

In the Creation section, we can then set the title and modify the embed code using regular expressions so that it has the correct width and height. Finally, we add back the iframe of the map to the target container with the `html()` function. We can then export the finished symbol through the Library in order to import it into other projects.

Compared to the conventional map symbol in section 7.1.2 with static values, this component now depends on inputting the values. We can accomplish this with the following script in the `compositionReady` event of the target composition:

```
sym.getSymbol("MapComponent").setVariable("title",
"Brighton Pavilion Theatre");

sym.getSymbol("MapComponent").setVariable("map",
'<iframe width="425" height="350" frameborder="0"
scrolling="no" marginheight="0" marginwidth="0"
src="https://maps.google.de/maps?hl=de&amp;q=jenners
tr+k%C3%B6ln&amp;safe=off&amp;ie=UTF8&amp;hq=&amp;hne
ar=Jennerstra%C3%9Fe,+50823+K%C3%B6ln,+Nordrhein-West
falen&amp;t=h&amp;z=14&amp;ll=50.953236,6.931193&amp;
output=embed"></iframe><br /><small><a href="https://
maps.google.de/maps?hl=de&amp;q=jennerstr+k%C3%B6ln&
amp;safe=off&amp;ie=UTF8&amp;hq=&amp;hnear=Jennerstra
%C3%9Fe,+50823+K%C3%B6ln,+Nordrhein-Westfalen&amp;t=h
&amp;z=14&amp;ll=50.953236,6.931193&amp;source=embed"
style="color:#0000FF;text-align:left">LargerMapview</
a></small>');
```

The above method is a simple way to create libraries with configurable components.

7.4   Edge Commons

The Edge Commons is a collection of useful, additional functions for Edge Animate. Together with a few of my colleagues, I have published *Edge Commons—Dirty Little Helpers for Edge Animate*, a library under open source MIT license at http://www.edgedocks.com/edgecommons and GitHub (https://github.com/simonwidjaja/EdgeCommons). Not only may you use Edge Commons free of charge in commercial projects, you are also cordially invited to get involved. If you want to contribute code or ideas and would like to participate in testing and documentation, email me at: mail@simonwidjaja.com. Due to its openness, the library is growing and thriving, and many new features were already in the planning phase at the time of this writing. To hear about the latest developments, check out my website or my Twitter feed (@ simonwidjaja). At the time of this writing, Edge Commons includes the following functions:

1. Advanced Logging (various levels and groups)
2. Configuration (external or internal configuration layer)
3. Sound (integration of CreateJS / SoundJS by Grant Skinner)
4. Adaptive layouts (different layouts for different sizes)
5. Data injection (injecting data from HTML into Edge Animate)
6. CMS Integration for Drupal and WordPress (by Timm Jansen)
7. Parallax scrolling (without code)
8. Composition loader (nesting compositions in any order)
9. Spotlight overlay (overlay for elements such as YouTube videos)
10. Speed Control (controlling the speed of animations)

In addition, Edge Commons also provides smaller helper functions such as centering the Edge Animate Stage within a web page.

7.4.1   Edge Docks

The website www.edgedocks.com, a whole website devoted to Edge Tools & Services, was launched simultaneously with the release of Edge Commons version 1.0. The idea behind this website was to create a central meet-up and resource center for Edge-related content. This was what prompted me, together with some of my colleagues, to create the Edge Docks platform.

This is basically the home of the Edge Commons. Here you will find several examples and actual projects, as well as detailed documentation. Edge Dock also offers many tutorials and news on both Edge Commons and general Edge Tools & Services.

> **Edge Docks**
> www.edgedocks.com: news, tutorials, component marketplace, and home of the Edge Commons extension library.

The platform features a Marketplace from which ready-to-use components can be downloaded for free (and also as paid content in the future). The aim here is to encourage a lively exchange of ideas, projects, and individual components. Edge Animate's symbols and project templates are one such possibility. These can be easily exported out of Edge Animate and imported into other projects.

7.4.2   Loading Edge Commons

Since Edge Commons is a JavaScript library, you can simply load it with the previously described yepnope function at runtime. You can acquire the various versions of Edge Commons on the relevant CDN servers. For specific URLs, including instructions for integration, please visit the website: http://cdn.edgecommons.org.

You have already learned about the simplest ways to load the Edge Commons in various examples:

```
yepnope({load: "http://cdn.edgecommons.org/an/1.0.0/js/
min/EdgeCommons.js")};
```

This statement can be used in the compositionReady event of your composition, for example. If you want to use other individual functions from Edge Commons, you must first make sure that they are fully loaded. To do this, use the complete function again:

```
yepnope({
    load: "http://cdn.edgecommons.org/an/1.0.0/js/min/
EdgeCommons.js",
    complete: function() {
        // Your code
        EC.centerStage( sym );
    }
});
```

If you want to run Edge Commons on its own server or use it in an offline project, you can also download the library as a .zip file from the CDN page and store it in a subfolder of your project. Again, you use yepnope at runtime to link to it or load it directly into the head segment of the HTML document.

Once Edge Commons is initially loaded, it can be used via the abbreviation EC. The core functions are provided directly through EC: EC.centerStage(sym). Logging is also one of the core functions, which I will introduce in the next sections. In contrast, more complex functions such as parallax and spotlight are encapsulated in a sub-object so that the call looks as follows: EC.Parallax. setup(sym) or EC.Spotlight.open(...).

7.4.3   Logging

This function takes over from where Simple Logging in chapter 5 ends. In large compositions with complex interaction, logging is a very important tool to keep an overview. Whereas the normal `console.log()` cannot be globally switched on and off and also cannot group the output, Edge Commons makes both of these functions possible. The following examples show an actual application.

```
// Simple logging
EC.info( "Logging with EdgeCommons is easy" );

// Different Log-Level
EC.info( "Message" );
EC.debug( "Message" );
EC.warn( "Message" );
EC.error( "Message" );
```

Besides the actual message, you can also define a group to make readability and order of specific composition components easier:

```
// Logging groups (available for all levels)
EC.info( "Message", "GROUP NAME" );
EC.debug( "one message", "subpage portfolio" );
```

The Stage Timeline now looks like this:

```
[ INFO | GROUP NAME ] Message
[ DEBUG | subpage portfolio ] one message
```

A future version will also be able to filter specific groups. You can pass any complex object as the third parameter, which will be clarified in the output. This option also applies to all log levels:

```
EC.info( "Message", "GROUP", complexObject );
EC.debug("Current symbol: ", "TEST", sym);
```

As already mentioned, you can globally filter the output for only output messages that are at least subordinated to the specified log level. To do this, you can assign EC.Log.level to one of the following values:

```
// No logging at all
EC.Log.level = EC.Log.LEVEL_NONE;
// Only log error
EC.Log.level = EC.Log.LEVEL_ERROR;
// Only log warn and error
EC.Log.level = EC.Log.LEVEL_WARN;
// Only log info, warn and error
EC.Log.level = EC.Log.LEVEL_INFO;
// Log everything
EC.Log.level = EC.Log.LEVEL_DEBUG;
```

Finally, you also have the option to define an additional log target. This can then be used, for example, when you want to redirect the log output into a DIV container or display as an alert window.

```
EC.Log.addLogTarget(function(msg){
    alert(msg);
});
EC.error("This is an error log in the console AND as
alert dialog");
```

Project

The files for this example can be downloaded from http://edgebuch.
simonwidjaja.com
Project Name: Advanced_Spotlight

7.4.4 Spotlight Overlay (YouTube)

Now I want to introduce you to Spotlight. This component is similar to the widely used Lightbox or Colorbox overlays. Such overlays allow you to provide a detail view for individual elements, such as thumbnails, that covers the entire page. The contents behind the overlay are covered with a semi-transparent area so that the detail view gets the user's full attention. A small X-button closes the Spotlight overlay. In the current version, the spotlight function is limited to displaying YouTube videos. However, other types of media, such as images, Edge Animate compositions, and other video providers are already in the planning stages.

Let's suppose we've created a simple composition with a thumbnail as follows:

Figure 7.7
A sample thumbnail image to activate the Spotlight overlay

To place the spotlight function in a click action, first load Edge Commons in the `compositionReady` event. This time, also load the relevant style sheet that provides the CSS classes for the Spotlight overlay. Center the Stage in the callback as follows:

```
yepnope({
    load: [
        'http://cdn.edgecommons.org/an/1.0.0/js/min/
EdgeCommons.js',
        'http://cdn.edgecommons.org/an/1.0.0/css/style.css'
    ],
    complete: function() {
        EC.centerStage (sym);
    }
});
```

We can then create a configuration object in the click action on the thumbnail that defines values such as dimensions and colors of the Spotlight overlay. We define `YouTube` as the `type`, which in turn provides the two additional parameters `autoplay` and `media`. The `media` property for YouTube is the video ID, which is simply the URL of the video: http://www.youtube.com/watch?v=92ECI8JmPn4. Use `autoplay` to specify whether the video should start automatically. Then pass the configuration object to the `EC.Spotlight.open (config)` function to open the overlay along with the video:

```
var config = {
      width: 853,
      height: 480,
      borderWidth: 5,
      borderColor: "#FFF",
      type: "youtube",
      param: {
          media: "92ECI8JmPn4",
          autoplay: true
      }
};
EC.Spotlight.open(config);
```

The final overlay with the YouTube video looks like this in the browser:

Figure 7.8

The Spotlight overlay (Edge Commons) can overlay and play a YouTube video on top of a composition

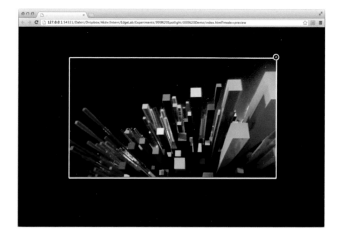

7.4.5   Parallax Scrolling

Edge Commons also offers what is known as parallax scrolling, in which different page elements move independently of the browser's current scroll position. Normally this effect requires an advanced understanding of code, but Edge Commons takes a very different tactic here, and maps the vertical scroll position one-to-one with the main Timeline of your Edge Animate composition. Thus, you can create any type of composition whose height is a multiple of the height of the browser window.

Project
The files for this example can be downloaded from http://edgebuch.simonwidjaja.com
Project Name: Advanced_Parallax

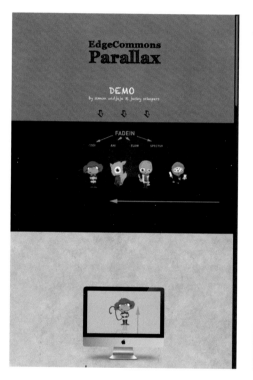

Figure 7.9
In the parallax effect, composition elements are animated in relation to the vertical scroll position

This means you can animate individual elements as usual with the Timeline and the Pin. With a little finesse, you can also visually create the timing of more complex parallax animations without having to rethink the code every time. The following illustration shows a typical parallax composition with the dimensions 1920 x 3200 px.

Figure 7.10
With the Edge Commons parallax
extension, you create your animation
as usual without having to worry about
parallax logic

Edge Commons handles the mapping between the vertical scroll position
and the playhead on the Timeline. The following script in your composition's
compositionReady event is all you will need:

```
yepnope({
    load: "http://simonwidjaja.github.com/EdgeCommons/live/
        EC.1.0.0/EdgeCommons.min.js",
    complete: function() {
        EC.centerStage(sym);
        EC.Parallax.setup(sym);
    }
});
```

7.4.6   Composition Loader

In complex Edge Animate projects, it can help to divide the project into several
smaller compositions. This has the advantage of letting several people work on
the same project, and it offers better control in deciding which content is loaded and when. If a user does not call up a large part of the composition during
their visit, it might be useful to keep this data outsourced to avoid unnecessary
preloading.

The following example shows two compositions. The composition "Outer.
html" represents the parent composition, while "Inner.html" contains the composition to be loaded with a text field and an animation.

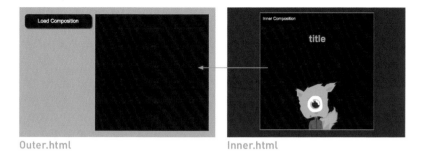

Outer.html   Inner.html

Figure 7.11
The Edge Commons composition loader
enables the nesting of compositions

In the "Outer.html" composition, the symbol named "TargetContainer" is positioned on the Stage. A click on the button loads the second composition. Once we load Edge Commons as described above, we can use the loadComposition() function to start the loading of the compositions:

```
var targetContainer = sym.getSymbol("TargetContainer");
EC.loadComposition("Inner.html", targetContainer)
    .done(function(comp) {
        comp.getStage().$("title").html("Hello Ani!");
    });
```

Via the optional function cascade, we can also add a done() function that executes as soon as the composition is successfully loaded. This function contains the comp parameter with which we can control the composition's Timeline or fill in text elements with text. Thus, this function not only enables the nesting of compositions in any order, it also enables them to communicate.

📑 **Project**
The files for this example can be
downloaded from http://edgebuch.
simonwidjaja.com
Project Name:
Advanced_CompositionLoader

Figure 7.12
The loaded composition seamlessly fits
into the parent com position

7.4.7   Sound

The first version of Edge Animate does not yet support sound. This is because support for playing audio is not yet standard across platforms. The Edge Commons sound feature is a wrapper for the SoundJS function and CreateJS library but also offers a simple method for playing sound in Edge Animate. SoundJS supports all modern browsers, and also runs on mobile devices with some limitations. Accordingly, this feature is still in the experimental phase. Actual use of the feature should be reviewed for each project.

The Edge Commons encapsulates SoundJS so that using audio in your compositions is simple. Before you can play an audio file, you have to convert it into an HTML5-compatible format (such as MP3 or OGG). The following example assumes that the two sound files were saved in both formats and placed in the project's media subfolder. Now at the start of the composition (e.g., in the creationComplete event), we can set up the sound files by defining a manifest for the individual sounds and their corresponding files, and pass this to the EC.Sound.setup() function:

```
// Load sound manifest (e.g. in creationComplete)
var assetsPath = "media/";
EC.Sound.setup(
    [
        {src: assetsPath + "bassdrum.mp3|"
            + assetsPath + "bassdrum.ogg", id: "bassdrum"},
        {src: assetsPath + "snaredrum.mp3|"
            + assetsPath + "snaredrum.ogg", id: 'snaredrum'}
    ],
    function(){ EC.info("Sound setup finished", "DEMO");
}
);
```

We define the two sounds with the IDs bassdrum and snaredrum. Both are assigned to the paths of the corresponding MP3 and OGG files, separated by a vertical bar or pipe character. Now we can play the audio in our project anywhere via the EC.Sound.play (SOUND_ID) function:

```
// Play sound (e.g. on click)
EC.Sound.play("bassdrum");
```

7.4.8   Data Injection

Frequently, external data is needed within a composition. Edge Commons offers the possibility to inject data into the containing HTML document. This can be done manually or through methods such as a CMS. This has two advantages: first, this operation is not asynchronous, and thus is faster than querying the data by a repeated request. Moreover, it is very easy to create reusable compositions that can be adjusted to the actual usage scenario via the simple injection of data.

The procedure is quite simple. Use a simple script block to define a JSON object within the composition's DIV container:

```
<div id="Stage« class="EDGE-189325992">
    <script class="data« type="text/data">
        {
        url: "http://www.some-url.com",
        user: {
            firstname: "Simon",
            lastname: "Widjaja"
        }
    </script>
</div>
```

Once the data has been injected, you can use this in the `compositionReady` event or within a click action:

```
// Get the injected data.
var injectedData = EC.getInjectedData(sym);
// Do something with the data.
alter("Hello " + injectedData.firstname + " "
    + injectedData.lastname);
```

7.5 Gaming

Edge Animate supports only fixed animations in the first version. In other words, the user can only use play and stop to move an element, such as a character. The Edge Animate API simply does not offer any additional functions for this purpose. It also lacks basic functions such as collision detection, without which a game is hardly possible. Edge Animate is expected to be extended to include these features at some point. However, the missing features do not prevent us from taking a brief look at the topic in more detail. In an experiment, I wanted to take a stand against a difficult situation and find out what might already be feasible with additional libraries under the current rudimentary technical conditions. I now want to present the results in the following section.

Together with my favorite illustrator, Jacqueline Schepers, I dared to do my first character design, the focus of our proof-of-concept project.

Figure 7.13
Jacqueline Schepers shows off the first draft for the proof-of-concept game

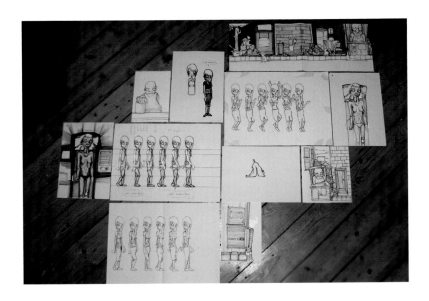

Figure 7.14

First draft of the game experiment in
Edge Animate

Since Edge Animate only displays content based on open web standards, it was clear from the beginning that rich 3D worlds could not be created. Thus, we opted for a two-dimensional scene to be explored by our character. In addition, simple hotspots should be created in Edge Animate for interacting with the character, and positioned in a WYSIWYG fashion at the time of design. Here, obstacles and actions should be differentiated. With this in mind, we created numerous snapshots of the character standing, running, and jumping, and a larger background collage that offers plenty of space for the character to explore.

Project

The files for this example can be downloaded from http://edgebuch.
simonwidjaja.com
Project Name: Advanced_Game

7.5.1   Edge Animate Project

Before we bring our character to life, we first create a new project with a dimension of 900 x 600 px in Edge Animate. We also ensure that the Autoplay Timeline checkbox is disabled because we want to control character actions via the keyboard, and not on the Timeline. We will only use this later when animating the game elements.

7.5.2   Game Assets

We create the background image with the Stage height of 600 px and a width of 1350 px, and place it directly on the Stage. Convert this image to a symbol since we are now placing all elements with fixed position in our backdrop and can move them together with the background.

Since the first version of Edge Animate does not support true sprite sheet animations, we need to create this manually. We already did this in chapter 4, so we can reuse it here.

For the walk left sequence, simply mirror the previously created keyframes and then set them as a sequence. If you name the individual sequences with labels ("left_run," "right_run," and "jumping") and add stoppers, in the next step we can manipulate each of these sequences with script and play them.

Figure 7.15

The background of the game scene in Photoshop

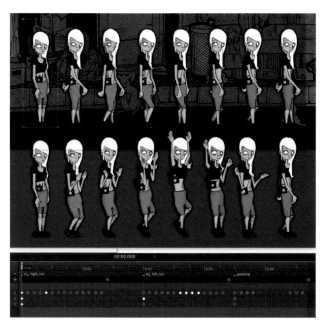

Figure 7.16

The character's running and jumping sequence

7.5.3　Character Control

Since the character needs to be controlled via the keyboard, we create a global action for the keydown event on the Stage. This is always executed when any key is pressed.

```
    function(sym, e)
1   // Animation Data
2   var offset = 100;
3
4   // References
5   var player = sym.getSymbol("player"),
6       playerElement = player.getSymbolElement();
7
8   switch(e.which) {
9       case 37: //left
10          var anim = playerElement.animate( {left: "-="+offset}, {duration: 1200, queue:false, easing: "linear"} );
11          player.setVariable("anim", anim);
12          player.setVariable("dir", "left");
13          // Animation
14          if (player.getVariable("state") != "left_run") {
15              player.setVariable( "state", "left_run" );
16              player.play("left_run");
17          }
18          break;
19      case 39: //right
20          var anim = playerElement.animate( {left: '+='+offset}, {duration: 1200, queue:false, easing: "linear"} );
21          player.setVariable("anim", anim);
22          player.setVariable("dir", "right");
23          // Animation
24          if (player.getVariable("state") != "right_run") {
25              player.setVariable( "state", "right_run" );
26              player.play("right_run");
27          }
28          break;
29      case 40: //down
30          player.getVariable("anim").stop();
31          player.stop("right");
32          break;
33      case 38: //up
34          if (!player.getVariable("isJumping")) {
35              player.setVariable("dir", "up");
36              player.setVariable("isJumping", true);
37              player.setVariable("state", "right");
38              player.play("jumping");
39              playerElement.animate( {top: -150}, {duration: 800, queue:true, easing: "easeInOutCubic"} )
40                  .animate( {top: 0}, {duration: 500, queue:true, easing: "easeInOutCubic", complete: function(){
41                      player.stop("right");
42                      player.setVariable("isJumping", false);
43                  }} );
44          }
45          break;
46  }
47
```

In (1), we get a reference to the player symbol we created earlier and the associated DOM element so that we can move this in the next steps with the jQuery animate() function. In (2), we can respond to pressing the arrow keys, and start the relevant animation. We save a reference to the anim motion animation as a symbol variable so that we can later possibly stop this in advance, such as for a collision with an object 3. We also use the state symbol variable, which is used in the loop behavior within the symbol, and move the playhead to animation sequence (4).

If the player presses the down arrow key, the character should immediately stop (5). In (6), we execute the jump. If the character is not yet jumping, the variables are set, the corresponding jump sequence from the sprite sheet is played, and the character is moved up and down via a jQuery animation, and then slowed down through an easing (7). If the player releases the key (keyup) and the character is not currently jumping, we return it to an at-rest position. Now the composition can be launched in the browser and the character can be controlled.

Figure 7.17

The finished game scene with active hotspot

7.5.4 Hotspots

Now let's take a look at the hotspots. Since we want to address all the hotspots via scripts, we apply CSS classes to all hotspots to create the interactions between them and the character. We can get these later with a simple jQuery selector. We assign all hotspot graphics representing obstacles with the two hotspot obstacle classes. In this way, we can mark off the scene to the left and right with simple rectangles so that the player cannot leave the gaming area. Actions that trigger an animation through contact with the character are assigned with the hotspot action classes.

📝 **jQuery Collision**

The jQuery Collision plug-in (http://sourceforge.net/projects/jquery-collision) is recommended for more complex collision queries. This plug-in provides detailed information on the overlap of two elements, which can be addressed via CSS selectors. The value returned by the plug-in's collision() function returns a so-called overlap object that provides additional information, such as the direction. In game environments, the direction often plays an important role in the collision between two objects.

7.5.5   Game Logic

The actual game logic, which includes the hotspot interactions, is done in two steps in one action with the compositionReady event, which is fired once at the start of the composition. In the first step, we select all the previously created hotspots of our scene. We first query a list of all our composition's symbols via the sym.getComposition().getSymbols() action. We run through the list with a simple each loop, during which we check each symbol for the CSS ".hotspot" class. We store all detected hotspots in the hotspots array so that we can access it at any time in order to calculate any collisions.

```
function(sym, e)
1  // Find hotspots and save in variable
2  var symbols = sym.getComposition().getSymbols();
3  var hotspots = new Array();
4
5  $.each(symbols, function(index, item) {
6      var isHotspot = item.getSymbolElement().is('.hotspot');
7      if ( isHotspot ) {
8          hotspots.push({
9              symbol: item, element: item.getSymbolElement(), isActive: false
10         });
11     }
12 });
13 console.debug("found hotspots: ", hotspots);
14 sym.setVariable("hotspots", hotspots);
15
```

The second step is a little more complex. Here the actual collisions between the character and the hotspots are calculated and evaluated. In case of a collision with an obstacle, the animation, along with the character's movement, must be immediately stopped so that the character never moves through an object. Through actions, the character can simply walk through something. However, the animation of each action is played so that, for example, hidden messages can appear. To implement this behavior, first load the jQuery library "jQuery Collision" via the yepnope() function (1). Once it is fully loaded, the callback is executed, which prompts the cyclical call of a function through setInterval(). In this interval, we can listen for possible collisions. Within the interval, we select the player symbol and the previously identified hotspot from (2). In (3), we now use the collision() function provided by the plug-in to determine with which hotspots (if any) the character is currently interacting. The hits variable now includes an array with the affected hotspots. We iterate this array in (4) with an each loop, in which we check what type of hotspots are involved (5). If the type is an action (6), we note this in an array in order to activate it further down or deactivate it through a play reverse when leaving the hotspot.

```
16   // Find hotspots and save in variable
17   //...
18   |
19   // Load jQuery Collision
20   yepnope({
21     load: ["libs/jquerycollision1.0.1/jquery-collision-1.0.1.js"],
22     callback: function() {
23       // INTERVAL
24       setInterval( function () {
25         var playerSymbol = sym.getSymbol("player");
26         var hotspots = sym.getVariable("hotspots");
27         var newlyActivated = new Array();
28
29         var hits = playerSymbol.getSymbolElement()
30           .collision(".hotspot", {
31             relative: "collider", obstacleData: "odata", colliderData: "cdata",
32             directionData: "ddata", as: "<div/>"
33           });
34
35         if (hits && hits.length) {
36           $.each(hits, function(index, item) {
37             var obstacle = $(hits).data("odata")[0];
38             //------------------
39             // Hotspots
40             //------------------
41             $.each(hotspots, function(index, hs) {
42               //------------------
43               // Actions
44               //------------------
45               if ( hs.element[0] == obstacle && hs.element.is('.action') ) {
46                 newlyActivated.push(hs);
47               }
48               //------------------
49               // Obstacle
50               //------------------
51               if ( hs.element[0] == obstacle && hs.element.is('.obstacle') ) {
52                 hs.isActive = true;
53                 var d = $(hits).data("ddata");
54                 var dir = playerSymbol.getVariable("dir");
55                 if ( ( d == "S" || d == "SE" || d == "NE" ) && dir == "right" ) {
56                   console.debug("suppressed right");
57                   playerSymbol.getVariable("anim").stop(true);
58                 }
59                 else if ( ( d == "W" || d == "NW" || d == "SW" ) && dir == "left" ) {
60                   console.debug("suppressed left");
61                   playerSymbol.getVariable("anim").stop(true);
62                 }
63               }
64             });
65           });
66         }
67         //------------------------
68         // Disable Action Hotspots
69         //------------------------
70         $.each(hotspots, function(index, hs) {
71           if ( $.inArray(hs, newlyActivated) > -1 && !hs.isActive && hs.element.is('.action') ) {
72             hs.isActive = true;
73             hs.symbol.play(0);
74             //console.debug("play");
75           }
76           else if ( $.inArray(hs, newlyActivated) == -1 && hs.isActive && hs.element.is('.action') ) {
77             hs.isActive = false;
78             hs.symbol.playReverse();
79             //console.debug("playReverse");
80           }
81         });
82         //------------------------
83         // Scroll Background
84         //------------------------
85         var levelElement = sym.getSymbol("viewport").getSymbol("level").getSymbolElement();
86         var playerX = playerSymbol.getSymbolElement().position().left;
87         var stageWidth = sym.getSymbolElement().width();
88         var levelX = sym.getSymbol("viewport").getSymbol("level").getSymbolElement().position().left;
89         var levelWidth = sym.getSymbol("viewport").getSymbol("level").getSymbolElement().width();
90         var levelNewX = Math.floor( ( playerX / stageWidth ) * levelWidth * -1 + 100 );
91         levelElement.css("left", levelNewX);
92       });
93     }
94   });
95
```

If the hotspot in question is an obstacle (7), we first check the direction of the collision via the `data` property of the `hits` object and compare this with the direction of the character. In this way we can prevent the collision with an obstacle from the right and the left by directly stopping the animation movement:

```
playerSymbol.getVariable("anim").stop(true)
```

(8) involves a few cosmetic adjustments in which we minimally shift the background dependent on the character's x-coordinate so that a typical game look is created. To do this, calculate the new position and then apply this to the originally set level `via levelElement.css().`

7.5.6   Conclusion

Edge Animate is not yet the perfect tool for game development since it is missing several key functions that effect performance, such as support for HTML5 Canvas or SVG rendering. For relatively complex scenes, this can quickly lead to a performance problem. However, a big advantage of this approach is that Edge Animate offers a visual tool for easily creating animated characters, game elements, and the entire level layout in a WYSIWYG environment. Anyone who is not an expert in game development will surely prefer this method to pure code-driven development with its many change-save-run cycles.

Index